THE TRAVELLERS' BOOK

OF

COLOUR

PHOTOGRAPHY

Van Phillips

Owen Thomas

PHOTO

THE TRAVELLERS' BOOK OF

COLOUR

GRAPHY

HAMLYN

EDITOR: RONALD SETTER
ART DIRECTOR: FELIX BRENNER
DESIGNER: DAVID WARNER

Published by
The Hamlyn Publishing Group Limited
London · New York · Sydney · Toronto
Hamlyn House, Feltham, Middlesex, England
© Copyright Van Phillips and Owen Thomas 1966
Fourth Impression 1972
ISBN: 0-517-089289
All rights reserved - Printed in Italy
Officine Grafiche A. Mondadori - Verona

Foreword

Cameras don't take pictures – people do. That is why we have written this book about *pictures*, not about cameras. Our illustrations are made from colour transparencies which could have been taken by any amateur with a very simple camera. We think we can prove to you that *judgment is more important than apparatus*. When you use your camera the main things you need to decide are:

what to take
when to take it
where to take it from.

The purpose of this book is to help you to develop this kind of judgment quickly and easily – because without it you will be disappointed by your results.

You probably take more photographs when you are travelling on holiday than at any other time. There are 400 pictures in this book, specially taken during visits to fifteen countries, showing well-known subjects of the kind that most travellers wish to photograph in colour. They are not intended as models for you to copy exactly – though we give many practical tips if you should wish to do so. They are meant to illustrate our ideas on successful picture taking. Intentionally, no exposure details have been included. We think they would be misleading, for you would rarely encounter the same lighting conditions that we did in any given place. You will

probably use an exposure meter. If not, you may safely follow the instructions in the makers' leaflet enclosed with every roll of film.

Good colour photography is now within the reach of everyone and there have been many books written about it. But never before has there been a book completely illustrated in colour and specially written to help the tourist take better colour pictures on his travels.

We hope you will enjoy using it as much as we have enjoyed making it.
Van Phillips & Owen Thomas

St Tropez

Contents

Segovia

Durham Cathedral

Mykonos

Dubrovnik

Copenhagen

Amsterdam

Framing the Picture

Use the endless possibilities of this device for change of pace

In our ten examples of framing we have not used the most familiar one of all – the picture taken through a doorway arch. Instead we hope to encourage you to look for other frames. You will find references in our captions to hiding a dull sky, dealing with a subject too far distant, the precise geometrical frame, the romantic touch and the humorous note.

You will be very lucky if you find the perfect picture every time – blue sky and white clouds, beautiful subject perfectly placed, no scaffolding on the church spire. So when perfection eludes you remember that framing might get you out of trouble.

A SKYSCRAPERS
This New York scene was taken from a twenty-second floor. The high viewpoint shows everything in the distant street on a microscopic scale. Compare the size of the cars in the street with those unexpectedly parked on the roof in the foreground. Question: do the two massive towers serve as 'framing', or are they the subject of the picture?

TIP:
your best pictures of New York skyscrapers will be taken from about this height; at street level you are forced to point the camera upwards with the inevitable converging verticals – buildings leaning towards each other.

B DUTCH WINDMILL
Our windmill in Zaandam, separated from us by a canal and a field, looked unimpressively tiny in the viewfinder. The frame of trees gave a romantic touch, helped to cover a wishy-washy sky and to obscure work in progress on a building to the right.

C

C PORT OF NICE

*The Côte d'Azur is noted for its sunshine,
but this is sometimes accompanied
by a heat haze which spoils
the distant scene for colour photography.
The gnarled branch here serves
the double purpose of concealing an
uninteresting distance and framing a
simple subject.*

D AQUEDUCT

*The arches of this Roman structure in Segovia
provide ready-made frames for your use, and are a
picture in their own right as well. There is a
noticeable stereoscopic effect in the relationship
between the arches and the two churches.*

D

A THE DANSANT

*The cloister of the ancient convent of Santa Clara
serves as a place of refreshment for Dubrovnik's
summer visitors. Displays of folk dancing (this one
is Croatian) are given at teatime. Dissatisfied
with our prospect from below, we went up on the city
wall – and found this charming example of framing.*

TIP:
*like other walled cities (Rhodes, Chester, Carcassonne,
for example) Dubrovnik features the walk round
its walls. Not all visitors realise that this gives an
opportunity for some of the best shots of the city.
(See also 54 A)*

B ARCHWAY
A very formal approach to framing, showing most of the Palais de Chaillot seen through the arch at the base of the Eiffel Tower. There is an almost geometrical precision in the central placing of the camera; only slight irregularities in the trees, cars and people break up a completely symmetrical view.

C WINDOW FRAME
The treatment is completely different from B. The Tower of London seen through an upper window of the Armoury has an offset placing in the picture space, and the frame itself has irregularities which prevent it from becoming a repetition of the outer edges.

C

B

11

*A picturesque group of buildings in
Bruges, not easy to photograph as it is
impossible to treat the flat frontage of
the Town Hall as anything but a frontage.
By including the Greffe du Franc
(centre), the corner of the forecourt
and the framing branches, we were
able to introduce a pictorial element.*
TIP:
*an angle or corner makes a picture
with three dimensions, while a façade
shows very little more than two.*

A

12

B QUARTET

As we say elsewhere, nearly all the pictures in this book can be taken with an ordinary camera with a fixed standard lens. This is one of the exceptions, taken with a long-focus lens. Snow White, at the 1965 World's Fair, stands well above the visitors in her amusing 'frame'.

C FAIR LADIES

If you have not already put the Spring Fair in Seville amongst your travel targets, perhaps this picture will persuade you. These two señoritas were not posing for us; strolling through the Parque Maria Luisa we found them prettily posed for their boy friends' cameras – and we moved in. Happens every day at the Fair.

B

C

Colour Recipe: Take One Blue Sky

A

Add white clouds to taste

It is hard to imagine an outdoor photograph which would not be improved by a bright blue sky and some fleecy white clouds. Whenever you see them, wherever you are, it's a day for pictures.

Look for an attractive cloud formation above your subject, and remember that the bluest sky is always in the direction you face when you have the sun at your back.

We don't suggest that you can make a picture of blue sky and white clouds alone; but look at our orchids, the cathedral and the Grand Canyon, and you will appreciate how much the brilliant blue and white has added.

A FIRST SKYSCRAPER
Although we have pictures of the Eiffel Tower with foreground interest or with people to provide animation, we here show the familiar structure backed by a sky which can really be called exciting.
TIP:
you will certainly want to take a picture like this; but while you're there don't forget the animated scenes round the entrances and staircases.

B VALLEY FLOOR
The extraordinary quality of Yosemite National Park, as in many other cases, cannot be shown from a single picture. From our Californian files we have chosen this one, showing the entrance to the seven-mile-long valley floor, between the towering El Capitan on the left and Bridalveil Falls. Approaching from Merced this is your first real view of the valley. If you are driving make a picture-stop here.

14

B DOUBLE DECKER
There are many pictures of Gracie Fields'
luxurious 'Canzone del Mare', and as many
of the Faraglioni – Capri's familiar rock
trio – but you seldom see them both in the
same picture.
We could have included all the bathing
pool, but preferred this version
with the clouds.

A

A DANISH BLUE
Before marinas were ever thought of,
Copenhagen's Royal Yacht Club was one
of the most beautiful yacht basins
in Europe – and still is.
On a fine summer day the traffic is as
busy as a city centre; you may even find
a luxury liner cruising inexplicably
through the trees.
TIP:
almost all visitors to Copenhagen go to
see the Little Mermaid. Few of them know
about the Royal Yacht Club, only two or
three minutes away.

B

C ORCHIDS
*This teaches us three things.
First: attention has been concentrated by
selecting only one spike of blossoms – there
were four. Second: to use sky and clouds
as a natural background the plant pot
has been brought outdoors. Third: the camera
angle ensures that the two ends of the spike
are equidistant from the lens.*

D SKYSCAPE, N. Y.
*When you go to New York you will visit
the U.N. Building. You will discover when
you try to take a picture of it that the
best shot is from across the East
River somewhere; we discovered it is from
the Pepsi-Cola docks. Phone the office
of the Vice-President
and you will get the necessary permission.*

C

D

17

A ENGLISH ABBEY
Since cathedrals normally run east and west, a picture of the great West Front will be an afternoon shot. Here the honey-brown stone of St Albans seems warm and mellow in the late afternoon light.

TIP:
the fact that our cheerful lady, caught stepping it out, is slightly blurred might have been held against us at one time. Nowadays such blurring is acceptable and even encouraged.

B GRAND CANYON
Both of our landscapes in this section are in a horizontal format, which is the painter's choice to express stability and restfulness.
This mood is emphasised by the long narrow cloud formation.
Note the clarity and contrast in the foreground crags and the softening of the colours receding to the distant walls of the canyon four miles away.

A

B

C SUNNY SMILE

*We met her in the cable-car taking us up
to the Vallugagrat from St Anton. To add
a touch of drama to her portrait we used
a polarising filter to darken the sky. Note
the slightly off-centre placing of the figure,
and the red lining of the gauntlet.*
TIP:
*we used the railing to help give the lady
that casual look. In another place a wall,
a table top or a chair-back can help
to answer the question: 'What do I do
with my hands?'*

D ROMAN NEIGHBOURS

*The Arch of Constantine has stood there
for 1,600 years but you can't stand for
two minutes where we took this picture,
in the Via di San Gregorio, because of the
endless traffic. The Colosseum is not
usually taken from this side, the lower one,
but we wanted it in the picture
with the Arch.*

C

D

19

Make for the Market

A kaleidoscope of colour on a plate!

Where else can you find such an array of inducements for the colour photographer?
Daylight in the open air, characters as varied as the goods they sell, colourful customers, historic settings, quaint costumes, animation and bustle. A constantly moving patchwork quilt of activity.
From the weekly market in the small village to the daily one in the big city, there is one to visit wherever you are – entrance free.
If you haven't come to grips with 'candids' yet, walk round the market first and select the most attractive display and stall-keeper. All you need now is the right customer to come up and haggle.
Make for the market, and take twice as much film as you think you'll need.

A   FLOWERS
This is the Monday market in Prinsengracht, Amsterdam. Any other day of the week you will find it full of parked cars, but you don't need to go to Holland for those. The morning is the best time for lighting, for well-filled stalls, and for recording the uninhibited behaviour of the shoppers.
TIP:
markets are most crowded when most worth photographing, which doesn't make things any easier for you. We avoided difficulty by finding a place where customers didn't want to stand – at the side of the stall. We couldn't see all the display, but could see the jostling people, the salesman and the bargains being examined, bought and sold.

A

B

B FISH
You will almost always find good pictures in Bergen's thousand-year-old open-air fish market, the finest in Norway.
Try to manoeuvre yourself into a position like ours at the end of a fish-table, taking in both buyer and seller, and with the masts of the fishing fleet in the background. No dialogue is needed here; the two hands tell us everything.

C

C REEDS
In spite of what we say in the TIP for 24 B this is a long shot. Our reason was that we wanted to have the ornate Gothic 'Schönerbrunnen' and the twin spires of Nuremberg's St Sebaldus as the background for our group round the stall buying tinted reeds.

21

A CHEESE
The man has not invented some new bowling game. Every Friday morning he loads cheeses on to this sledge-like cradle in Alkmaar's market. The loaded cradle is carried off by members of the Cheese-bearers' Guild whose colourful staw hats you see in the background.

TIP:
the guide books tell you to arrive there early – and everybody does. Then it is almost impossible to get within reasonable shooting distance unhindered by other spectators. By all means arrive early to park your car, but save some film until the time in the late morning when you have the best light, and the crowd thins out.

A

B

B ART
*Visitors to Montmartre watch the artists
putting touches of colour to their
never-quite-finished canvases; sometimes there is
even a sale, and the vendors are as
picturesque as the paintings. Lighting is a
tricky problem as the Place du Tertre is
closely surrounded on all sides by buildings
which cast foreground shadows at all
times of day. We prefer the morning.*

C

C ANTIQUES
*Mr Lars Lindqvist is presiding over an
auction of antiques and bric-a-brac not far
from the market place of Visby, in Sweden.
As on other occasions we chose a viewpoint
at the end of the platform; you see here
the auctioneer in action, his audience,
a selection of his irresistible bargains, and
even the auction sign on the rear wall.
Mr Lindqvist was kind enough to remove
his dark jacket so that we could show
his yellow shirt.*

A

A FISH

In Castello d'Ischia we have concentrated on the merchandise and not on the buyers and sellers. The fish are being poured from a bucket into a large tub, and we have broken the close-up barrier by going in near enough to count the fish. A shutter speed of 1/125 sec. – the slowest we recommend for markets or candids – was just not fast enough to 'freeze' the falling fish. The slight blur heightens the impression of movement.

B

B FRUIT

Although the striped T-shirt was staying at our hotel, a surprising number of other visitors did not see Dubrovnik's picturesque market scene inside the old town walls. Readers who have stayed at the Hotel Dubrovnika will recognise its balcony at the rear.

TIP:

in taking market pictures don't try to get too much in. Look round for the most colourful stall and make it your main feature; try to include a colourful character, whether buyer or seller.

C FLOWERS

The lady in the blue top-piece laughed at us at 9.30 in the morning, and told us to come back later. And indeed Oslo's Flower Market is busiest about noon when you will have many shots like this. With more time you can get sharper pictures, more accurately focused – but the essence of a candid is spontaneity and animation.

Most cameras will take pictures at three feet – but most photographers won't!

Breaking the Close-up Barrier

Are you hypnotised by your viewfinder?
Does everything in it look wonderful – until you see the result?
Ask yourself what goes wrong. Is your foreground too empty?
Your main subject too far away? Your girl friend too distant?
The reason is a kind of psychological block – we call it the
close-up barrier – which prevents the beginner from getting near
enough to many of his subjects.
Look through any batch of thirty-six transparencies and, if
averages hold good, you will find thirty middle-distance-to-infinity
shots and six closer ones, with not a real close-up in the lot.
The eleven illustrations in this section are not all 'real'
close-ups, for a definite reason; but notice the special impact
of the ones taken from three to five feet.

A MANNEKEN PIS
*Brussels' oldest inhabitant
is photographed countless times.
He's smaller than his fame may have
led you to expect, and you can't
embarrass him by getting as close as
possible to fill your frame.
Side lighting has made the fountain
sparkle against the shadow
behind it.*
TIP:
*try to plan your visit to his
quiet corner after 3.00 p.m.
when the sun first finds
its way into his little niche.
Before then high buildings protect his
complexion, and by 5.00 p.m. he is
probably in shadow again.*

B & C GRANADA
*The Court of the Lions is to Granada
what Big Ben is to London or the Eiffel
Tower to Paris. During the three days we
spent in the Alhambra we saw enough film
used to photograph a war.
What saddened us was the lack of judgment:
everyone seemed to be trying to get the
whole thing in – and became annoyed
to discover that it was impossible.
Our close-up is only one of the many
variations you can find if you
look for them.*

A CHINATOWN, NEW YORK
*Of course this is
not really a close-up, but it plays
an important part in this section.
We visited Chinatown on a dull day,
but were able to get a good picture
of this unique telephone box.
Remember that a significant detail
like this often makes a better
picture than an all-embracing
long shot.*

B HORSE GUARD
*Every day in Whitehall the tourists
photograph the Horse Guards,
but few will get a picture like this.
Nearly everybody stands fifteen feet away
in order to get the whole horse and rider.
Your picture will be different,
and better, if you step in fearlessly
to get this closer version.
The horse won't bite you,
and the rider is not allowed to.*

28

D APPLE-SELLER

*Frau Paula Birner,
in Nuremberg Market, is the
answer to a photographer's prayer.
Not only handsome and genial,
she positively delights in having her
picture taken, as you can see here.
Almost every market will provide
a worthwhile picture, but we
have a soft spot for the
one in Nuremberg.*

TIP:
*never try to take your first
picture of a stranger as close as this;
always take one from 12 or
15 feet first, and then move in after
'getting acquainted'.*

C THE SHARP END

*Every gondola in Venice carries
a 'ferro' like this one on its prow.
The significant detail once again; close-up
subjects such as this can be
found almost everywhere.
Taken from three feet.*

C

D

E

E SKI INSTRUCTOR

*In winter resorts, it is no accident
that so many of the ski instructors are
good-looking. Hans Niederkircher of
Seefeld made a splendid model for us
in this picture taken from three feet.
Note the simple but dramatic pose,
the bold colour masses
and the unobtrusive background.*

A BLOWER BENTLEY
*This supercharged 4½ litre Bentley,
once raced by Sir Henry Birkin,
was seen in a 'concours' in
Kensington Gardens. Our close-up
from five feet clearly shows the
excellent state of preservation
of this desirable property,
and gives a vivid impression
of dynamic power not so obvious
from a distance.*
TIP:
*the best opportunities of taking
close-ups of vintage and
veteran cars occur, not at races
or rallies, but at the
'concours' type of event where
you can wander happily amongst
the cars on display. Watch
motoring journals for fixtures.*

A

B

B NORWEGIENNE
*This young lady was waiting for
the ferry in Oslo's harbour.
Do you wonder
that we asked if we
might take her picture?
Although she is looking into the
camera she is quite free from
self-consciousness; look for the
moment when your subject is
completely relaxed – and if she
has a smile like this you've
hit the jackpot.*

C

C VINEYARD
*These grapes really were hanging on
the vine, at Avignon, and we left the
three grass stalks to emphasise this.
In working at such close distances,
focus as accurately as you can.
We took care that the two bunches
were the same distance from the
lens (best done on a tripod).*

The Fascination of Fountains

*Lovely to look at –
easy to take*

The fountains of Rome are as legendary
as the bridges of Paris; but other cities,
other towns, have their share. They come
in all types and sizes; the formal, the
ornate, the simple, the jet, the spray,
the trickle.
Visitors everywhere are attracted to them,
throw real money into them, drink from
them and, at times of great heat or
great exhilaration, bathe in them.
Those with time to spare just gaze at them,
those with strong political views meet
at them, those with colour film in their
cameras photograph them at 1/125sec. at
f/11. All are fascinated by them.

B GRANDILOQUENT
*Any travel brochure will quote the vital
statistics of the Jet d'Eau on Lake Geneva –
the height of the jet, the horse-power
of the pump, the speed of the water through
the nozzle – but you get no help about
finding the rainbow.
The right conditions prevail when the wind
is strong enough to blow the falling
water into a flat plume of spray while the
sun is shining on it almost at right
angles from behind the camera.
In our case it was wind blowing from the
south-east – sun shining from the
south-west – that enabled us to take this in
comfort from the Pont du Mont Blanc.*
TIP:
*you have to compromise between the brilliance
of the rainbow and the prominence of the jet.
When we moved more to the right we had a
brighter rainbow, but the jet itself was
hidden by the spray.*

A DRAMATIC
*The Esedra is one of Rome's best fountains
for the photographer. It is very large and
you will find it difficult to get it all
in – but why try when you can include two
such interesting details?
About lunchtime you will have more light
on Leda's face than we did; and wait for
a breeze, if you can, to open out
the central jet.*

B

C

C DECORATIVE
*Germany has a wealth of beautiful
fountains, but we have chosen this
little chap from Wiesbaden
because of the satisfying colour
combination of the heraldic shield
against the sky, the brownstone
column and the red geraniums.*

33

*If each camera click removed a milligram
from Manship's 'Prometheus' he would have
disappeared long ago; but few of the many
clickers in New York's Rockefeller Plaza
take the fountain from this angle.
Note the importance of the couple resting
on the ledge; we were pleased when
the blonde girl leaned forward, breaking
up the long expanse of dark brown marble.*

A

B

B NOCTURNAL

*There are two fountains in the Place
de la Concorde; this is the one nearer the
Hôtel Crillon and the Rue Royale.
This is an 'easy to take' fountain, the
only problem being to ensure that the
human interest doesn't move during
the exposure.*

TIP:
*the side of the fountain not to take
is the one where the ground is wet. Stand
there with your camera and you will
move briskly as soon as a gust of wind
covers you with spray.*

C SOCIAL

*Pigeons and people meet on equal terms
in Trafalgar Square. Although there are
two fountains the one we show seems to
be preferred by all parties as a rendezvous.
Here for once you can be on the
receiving end, and have your photograph
taken by the resident photographers.*

C

A

B

C

36

D

A USEFUL
*In the gardens of the Alcazar we were
resting on a tiled bench, like the one facing
you, when a crocodile of Seville
schoolboys came along and stopped at the
fountain. After we had seen this
little episode repeated by different pairs
once or twice, we roused ourselves
and got it on film.*
TIP:
*if you see a recurring event like this
you have the perfect opportunity to make
your camera adjustments first; then choose
the best actors for the parts in
your picture.*

B INFORMAL
*Drinking fountains exist everywhere.
The opportunity to photograph a casual
group of parched cyclists actually
using one is much more infrequent.
In Interlaken on a hot day we played a
waiting game – and won.*

C FORMAL
*Kensington Gardens are near enough to
most hotels in the West End of London for
visitors to make a pilgrimage to Peter Pan,
although many of them never see this
formal garden on the north side.
The fountain in the middle of the pond is
too far away to make a picture on its own,
which is why we linked it with the tub
of flowers in front and Christopher Wren's
Orangery at the back.*

D TRANQUIL
*You will be surprised to learn that
this little fountain in Seville was the
most difficult to take of all the pictures in
this section. To study the effect of
different viewpoints on the thread-like
sprays a tripod was used. We finally
chose this angle, for the best sunlight on
the tiny jets is emphasised by the shadow
behind them.
The yellow leaf was not there by accident.*

Sign On for the Night Shift

Don't put your camera away when the sun goes down

You can go out and take memorable pictures at night with the same film you have been using day. In one way you are better off; there's no need to worry about the weather forecast, or to wait for blue skies and sunshine – just go ahead and shoot whatever takes your fancy.

Our long shot, 42 C, covers the Champs Elysées to the Arc de Triomphe, while the close-up of the fountain is one of our own favourites.

If you haven't tried this before, you will be fascinated by the new camera world waiting for you in the city by night. It helps a lot if you use a tripod. To make sure with a worthwhile subject, take two or three pictures; we suggest 1, 2 and 4 seconds at f/5.6.

Don't waste an evening watching TV in a foreign language because it's raining; as soon as the rain stops go out and take some of the best night shots of all. (See 42 A)

A

B CAFE LIDO, AMSTERDAM

Normally we use the sky sparingly in our night scenes as it tends to be overpoweringly black. When there are some last remnants of daylight left we can be sure of some colour in the sky, even without the sunset of A.
Sign on early for the night shift – as soon as the lights are switched on.

A NIGHTFALL, MANHATTAN

Invited to the Cocktail Room at the top of the Beekman Tower Hotel, we were delighted when this colourful sunset coincided with the first evening lights.
TIP:
in our opinion the terraces on the four sides of the Cocktail Room are some of the best places from which to take the skyscrapers of New York. The Empire State (101 floors) is hopeless – too high and too hazy. The RCA Observation Roof (70 floors) is not much better; we waited ten days to get 198 B. But the terrace at the Beekman Tower, on the 24th floor, is high enough to serve as a perfect platform, and less liable to hazy conditions.

C CITY CENTRE

The overall green tint is not something we blame on our colour processors; it is due to the fact that all the light sources near the Martini Centre in Brussels are fluorescent, not tungsten, and such an effect is normal with this type of lighting. There is an interesting perspective lesson in comparing the relative sizes of the two lamp standards; in reality they are the same height.

A

A WATER SPRITE
This dramatic effect in Trafalgar Square comes from the underwater lamps, and is the direct opposite of the top lighting of daytime. A long exposure gives the jets of water an ethereal quality.

TIP:
you must have a permit to use a tripod in the Square; ring the Ministry of Public Buildings at Reliance 7611 and they will post one to you.

B

C

B FAIRYLAND

*Justly proud of their famous Tivoli
pleasure gardens, Copenhagen folk will try
to take you there as soon as you arrive;
be guided by us, and go in the evening.
A feast of colour and activity will satisfy
your camera's appetite, and later you can
satisfy your own at any one of twenty
restaurants – two of which are shown.*

C LAS VEGAS

*The clear Nevada night atmosphere has
produced an inky black sky and brilliant
detail right into the far distance. There
is so much light that the exposure can
be short enough to register pedestrians
and cars without apparent movement.
In fact, this is the brightest lighting
of its kind we have ever encountered.*

41

A

A   AFTER THE RAIN
*We do not ask you to take your camera
out into the Karlsplatz in Munich while
it is actually raining, but we do say that
some of the best evening shots are taken
just after the rain has stopped. The street
surface in the foreground would
have been dull and dreary when dry,
but now it glistens with colour reflected
from all light sources nearby.*
TIP:
*if you can stay in a front room in the
Koenigshof you will have one of the finest
viewpoints overlooking a busy city
square of never-ending interest.
Our picture was taken from room
310 while it was still raining.*

B   SIGN LANGUAGE
*The Chinese come into their own with
illuminated signs which to them read naturally
from top to bottom. The green tinge of
fluorescent lighting can be detected
here, but it is not so pronounced as in
39 C simply because there is not so much
of it. San Francisco's Chinatown offers
a wide choice of exotic subjects
night and day.*

B

C   CHAMPS ELYSEES
*You needn't be told that we used a tripod
and a long exposure – the streaks of car rear
lights moving all the way up to the
Arc de Triomphe clearly indicate that the
shutter was open for at least 15 seconds.
In visualising a shot like this,
remember that red rear lamps are more
picturesque than white side lights.*

D   FIRE FOUNTAIN
*Say 'Fireworks', and the English think
of the Fifth of November, the Americans
of the Fourth of July and the Italians
of Feast Days all round the year.
In Naples they think of Piedigrotta,
their very own September festival,
which reaches its climax in
a bountiful display of fireworks
seen to advantage across the water
of the bay.*

C

D

Catch the Passing Show in Candids

Think first - shoot fast!

By 'candids' we mean unposed pictures of people doing something when completely unaware of the camera. There is no time to ponder the choice between f/8 and f/11 or between alternative shutter speeds; all adjustments must be made beforehand unnoticed by the unsuspecting subject.

Having done the thinking first, don't stand waiting with the camera held conspicuously at eye level. Wait instead for the instant when the full story reveals itself – and then shoot fast.

Where do you find candids? Everywhere you find people, if you have the seeing eye. Not the flower garden, but the boy selling flowers; not the Piazza, but the people in the Piazza; not a static group of boats, but a lively group of boating types. No intelligent traveller's slide collection will consist entirely of candids, but it will be a pretty poor show without any.

A

A GANGWAY

It might have been the dinner bell or even a call to panic stations which made this lively bunch of youngsters in St Tropez jostle each other in their efforts to get on board as quickly as possible. Whatever the reason they provided us with an action group in which the strong diagonal heightens the feeling of animation.

B FASHION SHOW

These teenagers had just bought their hats when we noticed them in the Piazzetta in Venice. This is almost a classic candid – someone doing something, oblivious of the fact that his picture is being taken.
TIP:
in taking candids, all adjustments to the camera must be made beforehand; set shutter speed and aperture first; estimate distance carefully, and only then bring the camera into action. If you find it hard to judge distance, use the old trick; find an object, at the same distance in another direction, and focus on it. Speed never less than 1/100 or 1/125 sec.

B

45

A

B

C

D

E

A OPEN WIDE!
You may think that this animal in
Whipsnade Zoo is hardly recognisable
as a camel, but in the world of 'candids'
he is a major triumph. We ourselves
feel that a conventional picture
of a camera-conscious camel chewing
the cud behind bars is of limited interest,
while our 'grab shot' makes you *look.*

B WHO'LL BUY?
The shrimps in Oslo harbour come straight
from the boat to the customer without the
intervention of the middleman. On board
they are measured into the bag and
couldn't be fresher. This spot in front
of the Town Hall is always worth a visit
when the shrimp boats come in.

C GREENWICH VILLAGE
Washington Square is the place where the
unconventional young people gather in the
evening, and the edge of the fountain
is a favourite resting place.
Our couple were too engrossed in each other
to know that they were being taken –
and wouldn't have cared if they had.

D SWISS MISSES
Wearing their traditional canton dresses
they knew they were being photographed –
and looked liked it. When they thought
we had finished they broke into smiles,
and we snatched this one surreptitiously.
TIP:
with a group of several people there is
always a possibility that one will insist on

looking straight at the camera. Avoid this
by giving them something to do;
perhaps make one of them the ringleader
with instructions to amuse the others.
At any rate ensure that all attention
is focused somewhere other than on you.

E PIAZZA PROMENADE
The focusing technique used here
is different from that explained in the TIP
for 45 B. Decide upon a camera position,
focus on a 'firing point' and wait for
your subject to walk into range.
At St Peter's in Rome you will have
a rewarding choice of subjects at the close
of a service; before noon for best light.

A

A PRONE TO SUNBURN
*Along the coast road from Athens to
Sounion there are many of these casual
bathing-places, though not all have
such intriguing occupants. Your problem
in this kind of candid is not whether
the lady will object, but whether her
unnoticed husband or escort will.
In any case be quick on the trigger.*

B CHURCH PARADE

These are the traditional local dresses worn to church every Sunday by the ladies in Cilipi, near Dubrovnik; white hats married, red caps single.

TIP:

this a much photographed occasion, but it is sad to think that the hundreds of tourists who come by the coachload before the church service will hardly get a decent picture; the crowding and jostling must be seen to be believed. If you stay until after the service, the ladies then stand about chatting at ease, and you will have the field to yourself.

C FLOWER SELLER

This persuasive character was selling pot plants in an Amsterdam market. We waited unobtrusively amongst his customers and clicked the shutter when he was bargaining with a cautious buyer. One of the essentials of candids is that the camera must be inconspicuous or the quarry may lose his natural manner.

Whether you want to or not, you have to 'compose'
a picture. At the very least, you must select some part of
the scene before you to frame in the viewfinder.
Use the viewfinder *consciously* to compose the picture,
and decide where you want the centre of interest.
After you press the button it will be too late to do
anything about it.
There is an understandable impulse to 'get the subject
in the middle of the viewfinder' – just like aiming a rifle
at a target. Some typically unhappy results are: a view
of the Tuileries taken exactly down the middle of the
path; a landscape with the thatched cottage dead centre;
a picture of the girl friend posed centrally and,
of course, staring into the lens.
Once you start thinking about the position of your
centre of interest, many subjects will suggest their own
placing. A moving car or boat needs space to move into;
a portrait head (if not full face) is better 'looking
into the picture' than out of it; and a cathedral tower
needs sky above it to soar into.

Put the Centre of Interest Off Centre

You don't have to drive down the middle of the fairway!

A

A WATCH-TOWER
*While we were in Dinkelsbuhel the sun
appeared fitfully and without enthusiasm.
It was a desperate trek that led us into
the timber-yard where we could capture
this lovely little example of the towered
city walls, sunlit; we remembered to place
the tower off centre.*
TIP:
*in photographing any series of arches,
as on the inside of this city wall, always
try not to cut into the most important
arch – the one nearest the camera; leave
it fully supported.*

B CASTELLO D'ISCHIA
*Three mornings in succession we bought
slices of melon from this lady's stall by
the quay facing the Castello. One day she
was missing, and we followed the little
girl who went to fetch her. The quaint
exterior staircase made a charming setting
in which to take the two together – with
the melon-lady placed nicely off centre.*

B

50

C

C REQUEST STOP

*An off centre placing of the tower of the
little Templars' church in Segovia is
imposed upon you because any other
viewpoint will show rough fields with*
*unsightly debris. To get it all in you must
be down-hill, and you will then be grateful
for some foreground interest like our
horse and cart.*

A

52

B UMBRELLA PINES

The quiet little piazza at Anacapri offered us this chance to include a pair of tall umbrella pines. It would be reasonable for you to ask whether this is a picture of the piazza or of the pines; and it would be equally reasonable of us to reply that you may decide for yourself.

This was taken with a standard lens, not a wide-angle; but you must go right up on the steps of the statue at the side to get it.

TIP:

it takes a little courage to visualise a couple of trees like these as part of your composition; but looking for such component parts for your pictures will exercise your photographic eye.

A MIDNIGHT MONOLITH

The obelisk from Luxor in the Place de la Concorde is the main item both because of its size and its brightness; the fountain is a subsidiary note, being smaller and darker. They balance each other admirably; neither is in the middle of the picture space, and together they form a harmonious whole.

C BENTWOOD BOW

Between bouts at the gaming tables in Las Vegas you can revive flagging energies at the bathing-pool. The huge arch of laminated wood at the Desert Inn's pool is such a dramatic sight that you might be forgiven for placing it in the centre; but why not like this? The young couple would have been better a little further back in the picture, but this was a 'grab shot'.

A

A YUGOSLAV MONASTERY
*One of the joys of walking round
Dubrovnik's ancient walls is that you see
better views of many important city
buildings than from street level.
Our photograph of the Dominican Monastery
was carefully composed, placing the
tower well off centre. There is a strong
temptation to put a vertical feature
like this in the middle of the fairway.
Resist it!*

C PRICKLY PAIR

We couldn't keep away from the Arizona desert when we heard the intriguing name 'Superstition Mountains'. On the way from Phoenix we encountered these 30-feet-high Saguaro cacti; by getting two of them in the same frame we were able to suggest their unusual height by perspective, and avoided putting either in the dead centre so as to give a feeling of informality to these prickly customers

C

D PICTURE POSTCARD

The surroundings of this Dutch windmill at Aarlanderveen are not as rural as they might seem; only careful selection of viewpoint from a foot-bridge over the canal eliminated more sophisticated buildings which we didn't want to show. We placed the mill over to the left of the frame as we felt that more space was needed in front of its 'face'. The buildings on the right side make a balancing mass.

B

B PROSIT!

The Wine Queen at Braubach-am-Rhein's 'Weinfest' is Fraulein Gitta Dorsch. When taking this just after she had been crowned and presented with her cup, we asked her to look at the trophy, having made sure that we could see the inscription. This made it easy for us to place her head to the right of the frame, balanced by the cup lower down on the other side.

TIP:

when taking pictures of people looking or reading, it is sometimes helpful if you can persuade them to hold the object or book rather closer than is normal, almost as if they were shortsighted. In spite of any slight awkwardness the subject may feel, this will certainly look more natural in the finished picture.

D

There's more than One Picture in any Subject

Every capital city has one feature which the rest of the world tends to regard as an identifying symbol. Paris has the Eiffel Tower, Rome the Colosseum, New York the Statue of Liberty. London has Big Ben.

All summer long you will see visitors with cameras in Parliament Square, and you can tell almost exactly where the earnest photographer will pause, raise his camera, press the button – and then go off satisfied that he has one more good slide for his collection.

Inevitably there is a place where the viewer for the first time gets the full impact of the scene, and the beginner thinks that this is the spot from which the most memorable picture will be taken.

The accompanying group of variations on the Big Ben theme may convince you that there never is 'just one spot'.

56

B

B MORNING MIST
*Early haze diffuses the distant view, while
the foreground boats are seen in their
full colour. Sorry, but it means leaving your
hotel at about 8.00 a.m. to get one like this.
Taken from the South Bank near the
Royal Festival Hall.*

C FROM COUNTY HALL
*Another of the most famous views,
taken from the roof of County Hall.
For access apply to room 117a;
they are most helpful and
will provide a guide to take you
to the observation platform.*
TIP:
*go in the morning for the best light;
if you can arrange your visit round about
high tide you will be certain of some
traffic on the river. Note how nicely our
barge fits into the foreground and adds
colour to the scene.*

A

C

A RIVER FRONTAGE
*One of the classic views, and justly so,
from the Albert Embankment near
Lambeth Palace. The Thames is a busy
river, and you will always find a*
*colourful barge or sightseeing boat to give
life to your picture; our pretty little
yachts are only available on the day of the
annual Tideway Race, a Saturday in July.*

A SLATE AND STONE
A less well-known view, taken from
behind the statue of King George V,
with Big Ben framed between a buttress
of Westminster Abbey on the left and a
turret of St Stephen's Hall
on the right.

B ZEBRA CROSSING
Big Ben in company with several other
typical English features; the zebra crossing
with pedestrians using it, the
double-decker bus waiting while they cross,
and the Belisha Beacon
which indicates the crossing.

C

C BIG BENS
*If you like some light relief in your
slide shows, perhaps something like this
shop-window reflection will do. The tower
and its counterpart lean towards
each other because we had to point
the camera upwards. The shop is at the
corner of Bridge Street
and Whitehall.*

D

D TULIP TIME
*If you want to take Big Ben from
Parliament Square, remember that the sun
is not fully on this face until
after 3.00 p.m. If the river frontage is
the most popular view, this is certainly
a very close second.*

TIP:
*should you want to get your family or
friends with Big Ben don't let them
stand and stare at the camera; take them
walking down the path like the
couple here and your picture will
be more natural.*

A

C SUNSET

Don't despair if your day has been spent elsewhere in London and your only chance to take Big Ben is in the evening. Our picture shows that a sunset view may be surprisingly rewarding. Taken from halfway across Westminster Bridge; try shutter speeds of 1/15 and 1/30sec. at full aperture.

A EVENING BLUE

You won't see this effect in real life, but there's no reason why you shouldn't have a picture like it. Use artificial light film, after the street lamps are alight but before the daylight has completely faded.

B SIGNPOST

A low viewpoint is needed to link Big Ben and this boldly lettered sign on Westminster Bridge. Do you focus on the sign or the clock? We decided to get the sign sharp.

TIP:
the time of day these pictures were taken is no secret – it is clearly to be seen in all but one; if you want to know the time of sunset see your daily paper.

B

C

A

62

Doors, Portals and Gateways

An entrance for friends –
a barrier for foes

Consider the door.
What is it for?
To let people in;
to keep people out;
to make a good front;
to be knocked at by beggars;
to be battered by battering-rams;
to be bombarded by circulars;
to be decorated for festivals;
to be shrouded for mourning;
to be numbered for identification;
to have letters pushed through;
... and, like fountains, to be
photographed in colour at 1/125sec.
at f/11.

A   STILL GOING STRONG
*Today the stranger to Amersfoort is much
more welcome than he was when the town
walls and this gateway, the Koppelpoort,
were built over 500 years ago. The driver
of the red Volkswagen paid an unexpected
dividend when he saved our picture
from being just an architectural record.*
TIP:
*in spite of what we have said elsewhere
(See p. 50) some subjects do demand
a formal placing; if so, don't be afraid to
make it a completely symmetrical picture.*

B   ST CATHERINE'S GATE
*Of all the entrances we show, this great
gateway looks the most war-like. One of
the nine original gates in the wall
surrounding the old city of Rhodes,
it faced the medieval harbour and
figured in many attacks during the rule
of the Knights.*

C   BOEUF-SUR-LE-TOIT
*The Guild of Butchers built this 16th
century portal leading to the
cattle market from the Fleischbrücke
in Nuremberg. The inscription
on the unexpected sculpture overhead
says in Latin that this is the only ox
that never was a calf.*

A CHAUMONT
The best part of the day for photographing this château is about the time they close the gates for lunch. Fortunately you can stay in the grounds and take your pictures, although the way into the courtyard is closed from noon to 2.00 p.m.

B WHALE'S MOUTH
The world is not oversupplied with delightfully dangerous doorways or playfully perilous portals, so when we found this whale's mouth in Disneyland we went into action at once. Starting with a good one like this, you could build up a fascinating collection of bizarre, grotesque or amusing entrances.

C LADIES' PARADISE
No need to explain to a New Yorker
what this is, or where.
New York's two largest department stores,
with astronomical sales figures,
are Gimbel's and Macy's.
The entrance to Gimbel's was taken from
across the street with a long-focus lens.

D PROMISE FULFILLED
This 14th century gateway leads to
the ruins of the abbey William
the Conqueror vowed to build if he
won the Battle of Hastings. The field
itself is close by, and the little
town of Battle is a charmer,
with a wonderful 12th century
Pilgrim's Inn now serving as a
tea-room. Can you resist it?
TIP:
your best picture of Battle Abbey
gateway will be taken from
the inside; nowhere else will you
find such an attractive viewpoint.

A PHOTO CALL
Even the splendid portico of the House of Representatives would make a dull picture without the people – especially the group on the right, posing for posterity. If you're not in too much of a hurry you'll get a group like this. They come in the mornings, and arrange themselves on the steps of the Capitol about eleven.

C TRADESMAN'S ENTRANCE
If you look at the picture of Chaumont (64 A) you will see a small dark entrance to the right of the main archway. This is it from the other side. Note how the framing concentrates attention on the flower garden outside.
TIP:
it may sound paradoxical but the impression of sunshine in a picture can be greatly enhanced by including large shadow areas.

B GARDEN GATE
From a garden in the Alhambra you can look through this Wistaria-covered gateway and see the Albaicin, the old city of Granada, in the distance. The romantic flavour is strengthened by including the zigzag tiles roofing the arch.

66

C

With or Without a Body?

*Would your picture be better
with a human figure in it?*

There are many attractive landscapes which you feel
you mustn't miss; often they are disappointing in the finished
transparency, usually because there is nothing
interesting in the foreground.
When nature hasn't provided a foreground interest for its own
beautiful background, the only solution is to supply one for yourself.
If a shift of viewpoint doesn't produce it, then persuade
a friend to pose in a place which you select carefully
for your centre of interest.
Too often we see someone taking a picture of a distant view,
admittedly beautiful, but ignoring a nearby group of friends –
any of whom might have been used as foreground interest,
to the great improvement of the picture.
A human figure is invaluable to give life to a scene otherwise
incomplete, or as a 'scale' to show the size of the main subject.

A MATHER POINT
*Just for fun, put your thumb
over the group of people.
If you had first seen it like this,
would you really have known
what the picture is about?
An abstract painting perhaps,
or a double exposure? But with the
group brought back you are
no longer puzzled – it is undoubtedly
the Grand Canyon, and its vastness
is apparent.*
TIP:
*most visitors to Mather Point take their
pictures from the spot where this
group is standing. If instead you choose
our position on the rim, you will
be able to include a body.*

B

C

B & C TEMPLE IN RHODES

*These pictures of the Temple
of Athena at Lindos are identical
except that one includes two people.
The uninhabited one looks bare
and empty, and while it might delight
an archaeologist there are two things
wrong pictorially; first, the empty space
between the two sets of columns seems
to break the picture in half;
and second, we have no way of telling
the actual size of the temple.
Where the tenants have moved in, they
have helped to fill the gap between
the two parts, unifying the whole;
we can now clearly see how
big the temple really is.*

A BAIE DES ANGES

*The view over the Promenade des Anglais,
taken from the Donjon at Nice,
would be a very dull panorama on its own.
The curve of the iron railings, the
prominent tree and the two sightseers
combine to make a satisfying foreground.
You might like to consider whether a
better position for our couple would be on
the other side of the tree.*

A

B GENERAL SHERMAN & FRIENDS

*The departed warrior and his guardian
angel in Central Park stand so high above
the Fifth Avenue traffic that the
interesting part of the memorial is almost
beyond the photographer's reach. Taken
without the General's 'friends', the
lower half would consist of uninteresting
base and plinth; but the happy presence
of his visitors alters the character of the
picture, and now we have an interesting
and amusing slide for our collection.*

B

C

C WALL WALK

*The famous 14th century walls of Visby
in Sweden are well preserved and
extensive, but not easy to make into an
interesting picture. We decided to take
just a portion of them and waited for
this colourful group to walk into
the most effective spot to make a
balanced composition.
In spite of Euclid,
the part can sometimes be greater
than the whole.*

D DOWN IN THE MOUTH

*Although this setting, down in the great
funnel of Vesuvius, is so different from
Mather Point (68 A), the value of
the group of people is exactly the same –
to give an indication of size.
Blotting out the group with your thumb
is equally effective here; the crater
could then be any size –
thirty feet across,
or three hundred.*

TIP:
*if you want to photograph your friends
in the crater, you
must remain on the rim instead of joining
the party with the guide. Sounds obvious –
but easily overlooked.*

D

A YUGOSLAV PROMENADE

*This version of the Old Port in Dubrovnik
differs from many familiar pictures of
the scene. The main ingredients are
the same; the Port, the sea, the sky
and the Bougainvillaea – but we show
the strong diagonal of the road and, most
important, the little lady walking
on it. Here the value of the 'body' is not
in giving scale, but animation,
to the picture.*

A

TIP:

*most visitors to Dubrovnik want to
get a picture of the Old Port; this one
was taken near the Villa Orsula,
and if you want to include the road you
must ask permission to go on the
terrace of one of the hillside houses.*

B

C

B FIFTH COLUMNIST
Bernini's great Colonnade at St Peter's gets that lived-in look from the presence of the people. In a subject like this do be careful not to tilt the camera, or your 'converging verticals' will make Bernini's columns look as though they are about to fall down after three hundred years. More prominence is given to your 'body' in a sunlight-and-shadow picture like this if the figure is caught in one of the bright areas. Compare the importance of the walking man with the resting figure, larger, but half hidden in shadow.

C BODIES
We studied the Vigeland sculptures in Oslo's Frogner Park for some time before deciding that this viewpoint included the most interesting figures. But to photograph a group of statuary is merely to copy some other artist's creative work. We have tried to create something of our own by using the group for the basis of a picture with our gaily dressed charmer contrasted against the sculptured stone. (See also 125 E)

73

Silver or Gold *Show warm - sho cold*

Would you like an easy way to make
a dramatic difference in the
night shots you show on your screen?
If the answer is 'yes', buy a roll of
'artificial light' film from your dealer.
When we invited you to sign on for the
night shift, we said you could use the
same type of film you have been using
all day. Personally we do this ourselves;
but you need no knowledge of alchemy
to transmute gold to silver when
you take your camera out after dark.
We show four direct comparison pairs
of illustrations in this section,
which make a convincing demonstration
of the interesting experiments that
are possible.
All you have to do is put in the film
you have just bought and proceed
to shoot as you would with
daylight film. We accept no liability
for the curious, not to say nauseating,
results of using artificial light film
in daylight!

B

A

A SILVER GILT

*This is the odd man out in our series.
The newly cleaned Odéon Theatre in Paris
glows with its own natural gold colour,
and we felt it would be overdoing things
to warm it up still more with daylight film;
in this one case we considered the
artificial light type to be more suitable.*

TIP:
*although there was constant traffic
through the Place de l'Odéon you can
scarcely detect it. By covering the lens every
time something moved in front
of the camera we prevented it from
recording on the film.*

B & C DUTCH TREAT

*Sometimes still, sometimes ruffled
by breezes, Amsterdam's canals provide
endless entrancing variations on the theme
of reflections. Although basically our
pair shows the same scene on the two films
there is also another slight difference.
The silver one was taken first, during the
last minutes of daylight, which accounts
for the blue of the sky reflected
in the water. By the time we were ready
to take the gold shot all the daylight
had gone; we see no trace of sky in
the water, and the shadows round the
Cafe Lido are darker.*

C

A & B WATER PLUMAGE

You can photograph this fountain in
Trafalgar Square from any angle.
We chose this one to include the red sign
on top of the Coliseum. The clear-cut
separation between the feathery plumes
in both cases is the result
of an exceptionally still night.
TIP:
this pair were taken with a long exposure
and the camera on a tripod.
Moving objects present a special problem
with these conditions. People who walk
straight through your scene leave no
impression on the film, and you can
be thankful for those who keep still
all the time the shutter is open.
But those who stay a little while and
then move on are apt to leave
their ghosts behind them.

C MANHATTAN MIDNIGHT

Late at night on the observation roof of
the RCA building you will almost always
find a number of tripods ranging from
toddlers on the parapet to baby giants
five feet high. All their owners are taking
night colour shots, but how many use
artificial light film we cannot guess;
we ourselves used daylight film
for this shot over the Hudson River.
Electricity bills notwithstanding,
we get the impression that current is
cheap in New York.

D & E PAINTED LADY

Neither is correct – both are interesting.
Coldly analytical, we would say that
the silver version is slightly the more accurate;
swayed by our emotions we must confess
that we prefer the gold
rendering of Notre Dame Cathedral.
We found our viewpoint on the
Pont St Michel just by the Left Bank.

A

B

C

D

E

77

A

A & B PASO DOBLE

*Don't be afraid if occasionally you see
a mass of black in your viewfinder;
contrary to the advice often given,
the result can be very effective in suitable
circumstances. The immense Justice Gate
of the Alhambra can stand up to this
contrast although the feathery sprays in
Trafalgar Square would find it
overpowering. (See also 67C)*

TIP:
*while there is room for two shades
of opinion about the merits of gold or silver,
we strongly recommend that you do not
waste artificial light film when all
the light sources are fluorescent.
We don't think anybody would say a kind
word for your slide if you did; we dislike
the effect so much that we haven't
shown it in this section.*

Off-beat

*There's a place in your day
for a moment of madness*

Whether taking pictures or looking at them we are all glad
of a break in our normal routine. So much photography is in
deadly earnest that we need a touch of whimsy to brighten
the surrounding gloom.
This dotty note could come from an 'off-beat', like one
from our random rag-bag. Off-beat subjects are there all
the time, everywhere; the trick is to see them.
The full-blown practitioner of the off-beat would be
ever alert, studying all things from all sides, and with a gift
for decision approaching infallibility. But don't take
this superman too seriously, all you really need is
a seeing eye and an itchy finger!

A

B

A COIN CONSUMER
*Through half-closed eyes this might be
a try-your-strength machine, a barometer
at 'set fair' or the comfortable end of
a shooting stick. You know, and we know,
it's a parking meter, which is
just the loony sort of thing everyone
ought to bag sometime or other.*

B PARALLEL BARS
*Looking down from the terrace
of the Bellevue, in Sorrento,
we picked out with a long-focus lens
this musical comedy group
of bathing-huts and parasols.*
TIP:
*to add a touch of the bizarre,
frame your picture on the skew.
This would have been less amusing
with the two piers horizontal.*

C ULTIMATE
*This is the extreme example of tilting
the camera upwards. Pictures like this
are no longer startling, but in
New York it is hard to resist
taking them. Shooting from street level
gave us one of the Empire State's
more spectacular aspects.*

A

A DRYING FOR FRYING
Ostend offers cross-channel visitors
'Tea Like Mother Makes' and
'Bacon and Egg Breakfasts All Day'.
An attractive dish offered as
an alternative is chips
with fish which has been dried in the
open on wooden racks.

B

C

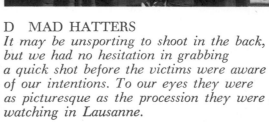

D

D MAD HATTERS
It may be unsporting to shoot in the back, but we had no hesitation in grabbing a quick shot before the victims were aware of our intentions. To our eyes they were as picturesque as the procession they were watching in Lausanne.

B HAIR APPARENT
The sun had gone home for the day, and we were about to do the same, when we spotted this trio in Copenhagen's Tivoli. They had no idea they were being immortalised.
TIP:
if the sun doesn't want to play, you can usually get something in spite of him by concentrating on a colourful close-up.

C HAUTE COUTURE
Without a blush we admit that we introduced the ribbon to the railings. There was the bow lying where it had fallen from some youngster's pony-tail, and there were the gilded railings just asking for something to break the monotony.

83

A DOCKSIDE DRUMS
*From the Fiallgatan, a hillside roadway,
you have extensive views over the
harbour of Stockholm. But extensive views
are a drug on the market, and our moment
of madness arrived when we spotted
below us this crazy composition
of coloured paint drums.*

A

B

B CRUSTACEAN
'How did that get up there, Mummy?'
we heard an Edinburgh child ask.
Without waiting to hear the answer we turned
to our knapsack for our trusty
lobster-shooter – and potted this
for your edification and amazement.
TIP:
in many places we have told you
to find high viewpoints; there are also
'looking-up' pictures like this one
to be taken from street level.

C   SEATING PLAN
This kind of chair is not our idea
of comfort, and may not be your idea
of beauty; but stacked in two piles
that fitted neatly into our viewfinder
we found them irresistible en masse
Taken on the Marina Grande, Capri.

C

Adventure without Tears

'I must go down to the sea again'
all passengers under cover in case of rain

How does the explorer best get to know
a new city? He can walk – and collapse
exhausted on to a hotel bed at teatime.
He can drive – and face
incomprehensible traffic signs, no available
parking space, and belligerent
local drivers cunningly playing on
their own ground.
Or, if he is fortunate enough to be in
one of the cities shown in our
illustrations, he can go by boat –
and none of these troubles arise.
Many tourists miss a truly delightful
experience through a tendency to dismiss
the sightseeing boat as 'kid stuff'.
How wrong they are could be explained
by anyone who has been on
a 'Bateau Mouche' through Paris, on
a Rhine steamer, or on one
of Stockholm's many sightseeing boats.
If you really want to get to know a city
nothing beats wearing out some
shoe leather, but the boat trip offers,
in addition to relaxation and comfort,
a special memory which the
knowledgeable traveller will appreciate.

A   VENICE
The gondola was once a business-like way
of getting about. For us today it is
a symbol of leisurely comfort and romance,
if a trifle expensive.
TIP:
you can photograph gondolas anywhere
in Venice, but not all gondoliers
are photogenic, nor are their passengers.
To improve your chances, stand on a bridge
where the passing gondola traffic is heavy.

B STOCKHOLM

*Stockholm without a boat trip would be
like a camera without a film.
The boats themselves are handsome,
and well worth a picture.
We took this from the Strom Bridge,
a ready-made viewpoint.*

C THE RHINE

*Without question one of the great
sightseeing boat trips is between Mainz
and Coblenz. This is no mere jaunt
round the town, but takes a whole day
to cover the 90 kilometres from city
to city. We chose to show the 'Bonn'
at St Goar, with the humorously named
Cat's Castle – Burg Katz – on the
opposite bank.*

A

A LONDON
Downstream past the docks to Greenwich or upstream to Hampton Court are the popular places to go. You can disembark and come back later on another boat or you can make a short there-and-back trip. Our high viewpoint was found on Hungerford footbridge, and enables us to see Shell-Mex House and the Savoy Hotel as well.

B DISNEYLAND
This is the nearest our intrepid explorer comes to tasting the true wine of adventure. Walt Disney's faithful reconstruction of a Mississippi Showboat thrills countless thousands who have never seen one of the originals.

B

C COPENHAGEN

It has only just left its pier but already this boat is making a fair rate of knots, and offers one of the few opportunities to get a picture of a sightseeing boat with some excitement in it. Forced to go through the centre arch of the bridge in Nyhavn where we are standing, boats come through at half-hourly intervals; you can have two bites at the cherry, getting him from the other side of the bridge as well.

C

D AMSTERDAM

As well as its extensive canal system, Amsterdam has the river Amstel, and sightseeing boats include both river and canals in the round trip.

TIP:

the canals in Amsterdam follow roughly a semicircular course with connecting waterways radiating like the spokes of a wheel. At some time of the day the lighting must be right for your chosen viewpoint. Try the Herengracht.

D

B

A PARIS
The grand boats on the Seine are the
Bateaux Mouches,
the others are Vedettes. At night you can have
a meal on board a Bateau Mouche and watch the history
of Paris gliding by, spotlit by the boat's own lamps.
TIP:
in this narrow part of the Seine between the Left Bank
and the Ile de la Cité, the boats move more slowly
than a walking pace, giving you plenty of time.

B INTERLAKEN
At first glance you might think this is a boat
with the blunt end where the sharp end ought to be.
In fact it's backing out from its berth to begin
its zig-zag trip along Lake Thun. The afternoon sun
gives side lighting
from our viewpoint at the Westbahnhof.

C BOSTON
These quaint pleasure-boats, gliding soundlessly through
Boston's Public Gardens, are one of the city's most
famous sights. Although the amount of sightseeing may
be small, the pleasure for both children and adults
is boundless. Take your swan-boat after it rounds
the islet on the right, when it is nearest the bank.

C

Don't let them Look at the Camera

Give them something to do

People are funny; unless they are looking fair-and-square at the camera they seem to think they are not having their picture taken properly. When your slides are finally shown to them on the sreen, however, they will be the first to tell you that you should have done the job differently. Don't let them look at the camera; take them in any sort of pose which directs their attention elsewhere – best of all give them something to do. Most girl friends would love to look like our elegant ski-girl; sporty types wouldn't mind embracing a nearby statue; tiny tots will put out their tongues and lick a lolly to order. Such simple changes from the stand-and-stare pose will result in much more interesting pictures of your family and friends; it is *your* job to give them something to do.

A   DANGEROUS CURVE
Although we boast that we have not used professional models in our pictures, we suspect that this elegant young lady we chatted up on the ski slopes was no stranger to the mannequin's art. Certainly no professional could have assumed this graceful pose more easily. We hope she never gets her skis crossed in a Telemark.

A

B

C

B SUPER-LOLLY
*In this case we didn't have to ask our
subject to 'do something'; she was already
doing it. A questioning nod to her Daddy,
and we had his tacit approval. Little Miss
Affeltranger had come to Disneyland
all the way from the Canal Zone.*
TIP:
*the simplicity of childhood is best conveyed
by a simple setting. We chose a low angle
to isolate her against the sky and avoid
a fussy amusement-park background.*

C BROWN STUDY
*'What do you want us to do?'
said our friends on the beach at Ischia
when we asked them to pose for us.
We told them to go on reading; it wasn't
a difficult role for them to play,
and made a natural and amusing picture.*

A HONEYMOON HOLIDAY
The Dickerhofs were on honeymoon when we met them in Ischia Porto. The little white boat with its yellow masts made the ideal resting-place; we had only to ask Michael and his bride to 'look over there' – not into the sun, notice, but enough for a three-quarter lighting.

TIP:
it is kinder to your subjects if you arrange things so that they are not looking directly into the sun; then they won't screw up their eyes, and can pose more comfortably.

C LOVE MY DOG
Karin Richter is a schoolgirl we met when we stopped to ask the way in the suburbs of Heidelberg. We wanted a picture of her with the Dalmatian, but he wouldn't keep still; we asked her to lift him up, waited until she had forgotten about the camera and then took it.

B TRESS TROUBLE
Two university students, Aase and Kirsten, waitresses at our Copenhagen hotel, were tempted away for a few pictures. We didn't have to find them anything to do; *the local breezes kept them fully occupied trying to control their windswept hair. What we lost in chic we gained in spontaneity.*

A

A FACE TO FACE

*We wanted a picture of this stallholder
in Nuremberg Market, and arranged
with her that we would take it when
a customer was being served. This avoided
the possibility of either person looking
at the camera; they were too interested
in exchanging pfennigs for fruit
to bother about us.*

B 'MIND THAT TREE-TRUNK'

*J. A. Bennett, from High Wycombe,
is pointing out a hazard on the run down
from the Ross-Hütte at Seefeld.
We know he is because we asked him to!
This is perhaps the simplest of the many
devices you can use to avoid that
front-and-centre look.*

B

C

D

D GIRL MEETS BOY
It was a 'natural' to bring the girl
and the statue together in Stockholm.
It would be difficult to take a bad picture
of her even by herself, but the combination
of the bronze gentleman's solemn pose
and the girl's cheeky smile rewarded us
for finding her something to do –
instead of just looking.

C BONNE BOUCHE
This is a simple way of dealing with
two people; they are looking at each other
and ignoring the photographer.
The shrimp-munching session in Bergen
harbour helps to make them
happily unselfconscious.
TIP:
with two people, take care not to get
one face in shadow with direct light
on the other; if you do you will
place emphasis on the brightly lit
face at the expense of the one
in shadow.

Purely Pictorial

There's always room for a few 'pretty pictures'

Many tourists live in cities and travel to get away from it all. To them the wide-open spaces are as attractive as any foreign town; a selection of pictures taken for their own beauty is as much a part of their holiday record as the sights and scenes of city life.

It is not easy to make a landscape look as interesting to your friends as it does to you. They do not remember, as you do, the scent of the new-mown hay, nor how good the beer tasted when you rested after a stiff climb. Your pictures can recall these things to you, but they cannot do so to your friends. To entertain others they must be interesting in themselves.

If you want your friends to enjoy your wide-open spaces, give some thought to picture *making* as well as picture *taking*. Even in the apparently simple 'pretty picture' there are guiding principles; we have tried to illustrate them in this section.

A COLORADO RIVER

Any group of slides of the Grand Canyon should include one of the Colorado River winding its way through the bottom of the Canyon, looking too tiny now to have been responsible for the world-famous phenomenon rising above it on either side. No need to tell you where to stay on the South Rim; you will certainly go to El Tovar or the Bright Angel Lodge. There is a need to tell you to allow two nights – better still three. It would be unthinkable to go there for less.

B ST TROPEZ

In the season the port of St Tropez is chock full of yachts and boats of every description; every one is a picture. This group was seen from the Môle du Portalet; the sky shows that it was one of those days when the sun is in and out of cloud all the time.
TIP:
if you use an exposure meter remember that these changeable conditions need a reading almost every time you take a picture.

B

A NUREMBERG IDYLL

Most visitors to Nuremberg make for the
restored castle and Albrecht Dürer's house,
but there is a much better picture
waiting for you at the Weinstadel.
Standing by the Maxbrücke you find this
setpiece composed of the hall, the tower,
the 'Hangman's Walk' over the bridge,
the tree for a vertical feature
– and a placid river at the base
for good measure.

B BODIAM CASTLE

This was the last fortified residence
to be built in Britain before gunpowder
made castles obsolete. Within easy reach
of London, on the Kent-Sussex border,
it is a haven of peace which the average
tourist does not go to see.
The exterior fabric is well preserved,
and it is everyone's idea of what
a castle should look like. Late evening
light gives a soft contrast, showing detail
in both highlights and shadows,
and emphasises the three-dimensional
effect of towers standing out
from the walls.

C STOCKHOLM

*We waited for the right day to take
our picture of Stockholm Harbour
and were rewarded with the sky and clouds
you see here. When you have this kind
of scene, allow plenty of room for your sky
and try to place your horizon
substantially below the middle of the frame.
If you can wait for a boat to appear,
so much the better.*

D LEAN-TO

*The few remaining columns
of the Temple of Saturn form one of the
prominent features of the Roman Forum.
They are usually taken from a distance,
showing the columns full length – and
upright. We have moved smartly in
and under, for two reasons. First, we added
drama by using the upper part only;
and second, we took advantage of the
only patch of cloud in the vicinity.*
TIP:
*intentional converging verticals
like these can be accepted, since no-one
would imagine this to be meant as
a straight-forward architectural study.
Do it boldly if you do it at all.*

101

A

A EYE OF A NEEDLE
The narrow entrance into Dinkelsbuhel,
through one of the towers in the town wall,
adds interest to this group composed
of the gateway and the town mill.
The scalloped gable-edges of the mill
are amusingly repeated on the sides of the
tower gable – a local fashion in this part
of Germany at the time when these two
were built in the 15th century.

B UNIPODS
These beautiful birds have been
photographed so often that they know the drill
to perfection. George, on the right,
has learned to arch his neck gracefully
into the picture, lifting his left foot
simultaneously so as to give as much sense
of stability as he can;
the others hide their heads
to achieve an asymmetric balance.

TIP:
in a subject like this where the depth
of field cannot cover right into
the far distance, the plane of sharp focus
should almost invariably be in the
foreground; exceptions are extremely rare.

B

C YOSEMITE RAPIDS
We travelled by coach from San Francisco
to Yosemite Valley, and took this picture
at the last stop before arriving.
As we started to take the river,
which here breaks into rapids, one of our
fellow-travellers had the same idea –
and we made use of him in
the foreground.

D MOUNTAIN GREENERY
You can see an interesting effect of
recession in the tones starting with the
green foreground grass and the more subdued
mountain-side immediately beyond;
the hazy middle distance is lighter still,
and the clouds and the snow-covered
mountains give a high-key note to the
far distance. For once the delicate blue
of the sky is preferable to a richer,
stronger blue. The farm buildings
and the people walking towards them
provide a minor foreground interest.

103

Stately Homes

Life with the nobility and gentry down the ages

If you have ever walked from the furthermost corner of the car park to the entrance at Versailles, it will be no surprise to you to learn that stately homes are amongst the most popular tourist attractions. Why this should be so is an interesting question.

Perhaps because we look back across the centuries: 'It's been standing here since the days of Henry VIII.' Or because we are overwhelmed by the beauty of the setting: 'Imagine seeing that out of your bedroom window every morning.' Or perhaps the sheer size of the thing gets us: 'Ooh Fred! Fancy cleaning all that silver.'

Whatever the reason, all over Europe francs, marks, lire, shillings and pesetas are being collected at the payboxes of châteaux, palaces, castelli, alcazars, palazzi and castles – a bouillabaisse of stately homes. Some are showplaces maintained in their original splendour, some are now museums, a few are lived in by descendents of the founders; all are worth a visit, and the reckless expenditure of colour film.

A

B

A CASTLE IN SPAIN
The Alcazar in Segovia stands dramatically on its craggy peak, a theatrical setting almost unmatched elsewhere. In the morning the light strikes the long, flat left-hand side which is the least interesting; try to take your picture after 2.00 p.m. when the light reaches the small turret on the right. If you must do them both on the same day, take the Aqueduct (156 A) first, at about 2.00 p.m., and the Alcazar afterwards.

B VERSAILLES
This enormous palace covers such a large area that only an aerial view can show its magnitude. Being temporarily out of helicopters we chose this small portion to avoid including extensive restoration work and filled in the foreground with the marble urn.
TIP:
don't let the foreground interest become the main subject; we have gone dangerously near to doing exactly that in our picture.

104

A WARWICK CASTLE

Still the residence of the Earls of Warwick after centuries, this is one of England's stateliest homes. Although the main approach is impressive, the visitor will probably decide that this makes a better picture.

TIP:

finding this viewpoint couldn't be easier; it's on the bridge over the Avon. We were half-way across.

B BUCKINGHAM PALACE

Built before photography mattered, this royal residence is still in daily use. Unfortunately the best lighting of the day wastes its bounty on the royal stables. Get there not later than 10.30 a.m. for the best light on the frontage. Even then it makes a rather dull picture on its own; we included the Victoria Memorial and the standard decorated in honour of a state visit by a foreign monarch.

C CHAMBORD

Amongst other features this famous château is noted for its immensely imposing frontage, but it was not feeling at its best when we were there. The far tower was encased in scaffolding for some face-lifting operation and we used the tree to hide this unfortunate blemish.

D RECTOR'S PALACE

In the 15th century the chief citizen of Dubrovnik, the Rector, was elected monthly. This was his official residence. The arcade in front has some of the most interesting detail in shadow. Don't be afraid of these conditions; we have managed to show the shaded part and the outside both satisfactorily exposed.

A

B

D

C

A   THE DOGE'S PALACE
The tapestry hanging from the balcony
for a film scene was a bit of luck;
our elevated viewpoint was not. We rested
our camera on the balustrade of the 'loggetta'
at the base of the Campanile.
This enabled us to shoot over the heads
of the people in the foreground.
TIP:
we could have taken the whole façade,
but by including San Giorgio Maggiore
in the distance and the Lion Column
we gave an impression of the Palace
related to its surroundings.

A

B

B CHATEAU DE CHILLON
*You will probably have the best light
from the deck of a steamer arriving
at Chillon about lunch time.
In our picture we had the
problem of shooting into the sun, and faced
it by finding a spot on the pier
where passengers disembark; at the same
time we were able to use the angler
on the groyne for a foreground interest.*

C

D

C CASTLE ON THE RHINE
*Marksburg is the best-preserved castle on
the Rhine, and much visited by travellers,
most of whom will not get a good picture
of it. The dramatic view is this one,
looking up from the river, and should
be taken with a long focus lens;
the 'landward' view is less interesting.*

D CHENONCEAUX
*Despite their colourful history,
the châteaux of the Loire are not colourful
in appearance. We were desperate
for a touch of relief in this view along
the River Cher, and persuaded
the adventurous mariner to manoeuvre
his craft into a suitable place. He risked
official rebuke by landing in the grounds
from the water instead of paying
to come in by the gate, just to oblige us.*

109

Variations on a Theme

*An exercise in searching for
the less obvious*

For the photographs on the back of the jacket of this book we spent two full days in the Place de la Concorde and took over two hundred pictures. Anything in the Place was fair game, but we avoided the more obvious shots – the obelisk or the fountains full face.

Our section 'There's more than One Picture' showed illustrations in all of which Big Ben was featured. Here is another group, also linked by a common theme – but with a difference. Although all the pictures were taken in the Place de la Concorde, each one is in fact a picture of a different subject. Viewed collectively they give a better impression of the Place than any single photograph possibly could.

The standard holiday scenes are there waiting to be taken and you must have them – but learn to look for the less obvious as well.

B

A

C DOUBLE VISION
*Framing the two equestrian statues
in the gilded spectacles needed some
careful manipulation of the camera to get
everything just so.
This is the kind
of picture where a tripod is
really necessary.*

A VANISHING POINT
*One of the easiest variations
is a crazy angle shot of the central feature
taken at night. We are not obelisk-fanciers
ourselves, but must admit that this one,
floodlit, is a fairly glamorous specimen.
Both this and 113 D were taken
on daylight film.*

B SIGN LANGUAGE
*As we say elsewhere, street signs of all
kinds are useful and amusing additions
to your pictures of foreign places. The ones
at home are too familiar to matter;
but abroad the shape, the colour,
the inscriptions are all intriguing –
NA and NM must mean something
to a Parisian!*
TIP:
*this kind of thing will be more effective
if you almost fill the frame. As you see,
we stood under and pointed up –
and didn't worry about the angle.*

C

A SPLASH

*We set out to get a picture of the splash,
and leave it to you to decide whether
or not we succeeded. This is not
a difficult one to take, provided that
leaning too far over with your camera
does not produce one splash too many.*
TIP:
*the shutter speed for running water
as close as this should be 1/125sec. –
faster than the 1/60sec. recommended
for normal distances.*

A

112

B C

C SHOWER BATH
There are two fountains in the Place,
with a multitude of figures round the bases.
These provide plenty of chances
to make individual character studies.
Late afternoon sun emphasises the
bronze tones of the two sheltering matrons
whose plaintive demeanour seems to ask:
'Will it never stop?'

B CAREFREE
The Place is as full of sweethearts
and honeymooners as any well-loved square
in any other city; we found these two
dabbling their toes in the cool water
on a hot July day. We asked him to swing
his bare feet over on our side, and took up
a position where we could see the couple
nicely placed between the two dark
bronze details.

D FIRE-FIGHTER
What you see on your screen is not
always what you thought
you were taking, especially at night;
is this a marine monster in an off-shore
cavern? A fire-fighter in action?
A circus artist in the glare of spotlights?
Certainly a change from the same thing
taken in daylight.

D

A

A GILT EDGED

The gilded railings which prevent the more exhilarated from scaling the heights of the obelisk on Bastille Day are a source of inspiration. We stood close to the railings to dramatise the perspective which ends just where the boys are standing.

B

B CHAIR PAIR

We don't mind admitting that we encouraged these chairs to assume their sociable positions; further we confess that in a moment of inspiration we threw the discarded cigarette packet into place. We make no proprietary claim on the pedestrian's shadow.

TIP:
don't shy at stage-managing a little scene like this. Try to offer something to stimulate the imagination of your slide-show audience.

C RAGS TO RICHES

Is this another millionaire in the making? We found him selling newspapers and encouraged him to put some action into it. The couple were fortuitous; they didn't want to buy a paper – they wanted to know the way to the Faubourg St Honoré.

The Human Element

Picture the people as well as the places

You are on holiday abroad. You are taking excellent pictures of cathedrals. You are taking superb pictures of fountains. In short, you are getting all the standard subjects waiting there to be taken; but have you forgotten the human element?

We have already invited you to 'Make for the Market' and 'Capture the Passing Show in Candids.' Now we remind you that people going about their everyday jobs make some of the most fascinating holiday records, a fact too often overlooked by the photographer. Try to find local craftsmen – a Black Forest wood carver, an Amsterdam diamond cutter, a Lapp shoe pedlar – for example; they will help you recapture your holidays more vividly than a monotonous succession of static 'pretty pictures'.

A SHOE-MAKER
Nikolai Antonsen makes and sells moccasins in Trondheim market. His amused smile has a simple explanation; he was pleased to have his picture taken! We sent him one like this (we always try to keep our promises).

116

B SHOWMAN

*When is a waiter not a waiter? When he is
a proud exhibitor. And Luigi Tognoni,
at the Transatlantico in Naples,
has every reason to be proud of his grapes.
You can take this big close-up with
a simple camera, but note that the grapes
are held to the side; avoid distortion by
keeping his head and hands in the
same plane.*

C DIAMOND CUTTER

*'Diamonds are for ever', and this cutter
is giving an extra glitter to eternity.
There is a friendly atmosphere all
over Holland, and permission was freely
given to use flashlight when we made the
ritual tour of the Van Moppes works
in Amsterdam.*
TIP:
*on your sight-seeing indoors take a small
pocket flash-gun and some blue bulbs;
you may get an opportunity
– and permission – to use them.*

B

C

117

A   STUDENTS
University students in Madrid
occasionally don these
troubadour costumes in the evening,
serenading the terrace cafes and
collecting for student charities.
We persuaded this colourful trio to meet
us one morning in full regalia;
our rendezvous was in the grounds
of the Prado.

B   WOOD CARVER
Wolfram Müller follows a traditional
Black Forest craft at Lake Titisee.
There was enough daylight coming through
his workshop window for us to be able
to take his picture without flash.

D SCHOOLBOY
*We came across Sammy Alvarez in
Central Park, N.Y., on a hot July day,
and he seemed to us to represent all
schoolboys of his age in all countries.
He was a remarkably good subject
because of his relaxed casual air and his
complete lack of self-consciousness.*

C AUTHOR WITH READER
*The statue of Hans Christian Andersen
is a fairly new arrival outside the City Hall
in Copenhagen, but has already become
a traditional picture-pal for the
younger generation.*
TIP:
*the light will not be any use until
after 3.00 p.m.; if there's no child around
you won't have long to wait.*

A FISHERMAN
*About to board the steamer back to
Naples from Capri, we spotted our friend
at his mending. He was nicely placed for
our picture, and too busy to notice us;
not everyone in Capri is on holiday!*

B DECK HAND
*Many people might think that acting
as crew on a Riviera charter boat
could scarcely be called 'work';
like any other job it has its drawbacks
and its rewards. This crew member swam
from the boat in Cannes harbour
to make fast the mooring line to the buoy,
and we caught him in the act.
That was work to him; perhaps
he thinks a photographer has
an easy life.*

B

C

C WATER CARRIER
*Women come daily to the old well-head
in Hvar and carry water away in buckets
balanced on their heads; although no doubt
they regard it as a chore, it is picturesque
to watch. Children learn the trade
by using smaller vessels – enamel jugs.*

TIP:
*look for places like this well-head,
where you can be certain of local colour
in action; when you are ready it is only
a question of waiting for the right person
and the right moment.*

A

One man said: 'They go straight up and end in a point. So what.' The other said: 'A spire is a church's crowning glory – a symbol of man's aspiration.'
The travellers we meet seem to range between these two extremes, but most of them are to be found pointing their cameras skywards from time to time. We think people take pictures of towers and spires for very good reasons. Sometimes they are dramatically lit. Sometimes there is sheer beauty for all but the Philistine to see. Sometimes the architect has thrown in a note of humour. Almost always there is a challenge, for towers and spires are never easy to photograph well.

Dreaming, romantic and utilitarian

Towers and Spires

A MONUMENTAL
The Campanile in the Piazza San Marco is 324 feet high, so that you need to be a long way back to get it all in. Fortunately the Piazza is 870 feet long, and you must use all of that to do the job properly. Late afternoon sunshine is the most promising.
TIP:
the pigeons are fed twice daily, at 9.00 a.m. and 2.00 p.m. From this end of the Piazza it is a remarkable sight to see masses of them in the air at once.

B SENTIMENTAL
The gleaming white wooden spire of the Memorial Chapel at Harvard needs no help from the photographer to appear a thing of grace and beauty. The setting amongst the trees against the clear blue sky was deliberately chosen to isolate the spire and to make it a picture in its own right.

B

122

A ORIENTAL
This exotic little decoration on one end of the roof of the Chinese Theatre in Copenhagen's Tivoli is obviously inspired by the pagoda of the East. The performances in the theatre are strictly European.

B ORNAMENTAL
We say elsewhere 'Do it boldly, if you do it at all', and this angle shot is an example of what we mean. If you stop at Split, in Yugoslavia, don't miss Trogir nearby – a living museum of medieval architecture. This is the Renaissance spire of the Romanesque cathedral.

C IMPEDIMENTAL
This splendid watch-tower stands over one of the old city wall gateways in Freiburg-im-Breisgau. We were fighting a losing battle with the traffic when kindly Herr Robcke hailed us from his first-floor balcony and invited us up – where we got our picture in comfort from a better viewpoint.

D INCIDENTAL
*Like Topsy, the belfry in Bruges
'just growed', and looks frighteningly
unstable at first sight. It is another of the
difficult towers to photograph and has
to be tackled from a far corner of the
Grande Place, preferably in the
late afternoon; even then the surrounding
buildings cast long shadows over
your foreground.*
TIP:
*if you have to tilt the camera upwards
to get it all in, exclude as much
as possible of the other lower buildings;
then your converging verticals will not
be so noticeable.*

E ELEMENTAL
*The two 'musts' in Oslo are the Viking
Ships and the Vigeland Sculptures.
In Frogner Park, just outside the city,
you will find hundreds of sculptures
in stone and bronze in their permanent
outdoor home. You will probably agree
with us that the centrepiece,
this 40-foot monolith, is the target for
your camera. In all our travels we have
seen nothing like it. (See also 73 B)*

D   E

125

A EXPERIMENTAL
Stockholm's City Hall, in spite of local pride, seems to us a fairly stolid and heavy-going structure; the architect clearly thought it a good idea to add a touch of humour in the form of this graceful minaret. Taken with a long-focus lens.

B SACRAMENTAL
This church at Philerimos, Rhodes, has a squat, solid looking tower decorated with the cross of the Crusaders by whom it was built. The caretaker monk who acted as our guide was kind enough to stand by the wall to indicate the massive proportions of the building.

C TRANSCENDENTAL
The pride of Seville is her great cathedral (231 B), of which the most prominent feature is the Giralda Tower. One of the important surviving examples of Arabic architecture, the tower was built in the 12th century; it provides the best views over Seville.

TIP:
this is the only standpoint from which you can take the tower free from telephone wires; stand with your back to the wall of the Alcazar.

Planning Ahead

Be in the right place at the right time

You may not be in Seville for the Spring Fair, or in London for
the Queen's Birthday, but whatever country you visit there are local festivals
taking place throughout the summer. Some of the most charming of these
are so tiny they don't appear in the national 'Calendar of Events'.
Ask at the local bureau if there is to be a 'fiesta' anywhere nearby;
with luck you may get some unique pictures, and later enjoy hearing
a friend's plaintive: 'But I didn't know it was happening.'
The apparently simple picture often needs a certain amount of planning.
The château is closed during lunchtime; the museum doesn't open
on Mondays; arriving sometime after lunch you find the sun was right
in the morning; crowds keep you from reaching a place to take the parade.
Minor frustrations like these cannot all be avoided, but you will make life
easier with a little forethought and planning.

A GRAND CANYON
*This picture required careful planning.
In summer eight or ten of these mule
trains go down into the Canyon every day
at about 9.30 a.m. – a better time
for lighting than 5.30 p.m.
when they return. We had to make
an early start to walk to our
chosen viewpoint a mile down
the Bright Angel Trail before
the first mule arrived. You may find
a spot you like better, but it won't
be much use if you get there after the
last train has gone.*
TIP:
*you will find U-bends like this on most
mountain paths or trails; if you stand at
the apex your subject, no matter
from which direction he comes,
must move towards the camera.*

B GRAND' PLACE
*The newly cleaned Hôtel de Ville
in Brussels is now at its best for
colour photography, but was not built
with cameras in mind; the sun only
reaches this face early in the morning.
In Brussels start your picture day
here to make the most of the favourable
light. For once we found the Place
free from parked cars because a procession
had passed through, but the delay made us
lose the sun on the frontage ourselves.*

A

129

C *ROYAL RIDE*
*Every visitor to London would like
to get a picture of the Queen.
She makes few regular public appearances,
but from time to time there are state
occasions when she drives through
the Mall in an open carriage;
you are free to use your camera at will.
Study the day's events in
London newspapers; or get a copy of
the weekly 'What's On'.*
TIP:
*naturally you will want to show
the Queen's face, but she may not be looking
your way; if she isn't, take your picture
early to show her profile.
If you wait until she is passing, you may
see only the back of her head.*

A

B

A FAIR IN SEVILLE
*The great Spring Fair is the most colourful
of such events in the entire world.
The only 'planning' involved is making sure
you are there during the four days
of the Fair; after that it's just an
embarrassment of riches – pictures
everywhere you look, and no doubts
about the weather. (See also 162 B)*

B LINCOLN MEMORIAL
*Although Abraham Lincoln sits in his chair
all day, in Washington, you must be there
promptly at opening time, 9.00 a.m., if you
want a daylight picture like this one;
the light worsens from then on. You may
find him easier to photograph at night,
when he is brilliantly floodlit.*

C

D

D TIDDLEY-OM-POM-POM

*We travelled overnight from London
to Geneva and on to Lausanne specially
for a procession in traditional dress.
Arrive early at all such events and get
a place in the front row of spectators
so that you can be sure of an
uninterrupted view. We used
our 'pre-focusing' technique; pick in advance
the spot for your moving subject
to reach when you shoot.
(See also 47 E)*

A TIDEWAY RACE
This is an annual event when the
yachts sail down to the Tower of London,
beach there for lunch and return
to Putney on the flood tide.
The best viewpoints for lighting
are on the south side of the river,
but much of this bank is built up and not
readily accessible to the public.
Find a sympathetic gate-keeper whom you
can charm into letting you stand on
the dockside; we even found a caretaker
who made us a cup of tea.
TIP:
a very good opportunity for
yachting pictures is just before the
starting gun when all the competitors
are crowded together jockeying
for position.

B ISLE OF GREECE
Mykonos is a magical name in travel
brochures, and the windmill of local type
identifies it in many pictures. This one
is a working mill, and if you want
a picture of the miller carrying a sack
of flour to the donkey you must be there by
9.30 a.m., before the shadow on the right
starts to cover the doorway.

C CHAIR LIFT
Pictures like this are fairly common,
but they are not as easy to take as you
might think. At the bottom or the top
of the line your subject will not be
high enough. Unless you travel your own
'Snow-Trac' it is difficult to get to a
standpoint midway. At Seefeld it is simple;
ride to the top of Gschwandtkopf II,
and take all the pictures you want of skiers
going by on Gschwandtkopf I.

D LOOK HERE!
Taken from our window on the top floor
of the New Weston Hotel,
this further illustrates the value
of a high viewpoint in photographing
skyscrapers. (See also 38 A).
In New York, especially, don't choose
your room as a place only to sleep;
your camera would like you to be in a
corner room, about the 20th floor.

Upon Reflection...

A strange, glamorous, topsyturvy world

Because colour photography is the perfect medium for recording crisp
detail and fast movement too quick for the eye to isolate, the possibilities
of the camera when used imaginatively are often ignored.
Simple variations from stark reality can be the starting point
for a new experience with the photographic process. Take reflections:
in some of our examples they are used simply to embellish the
main subject, while in others the subject is of less importance
than the reflection. The third stage is reached when the reflections
become an end in themselves.
Large stretches of water make the ideal reflecting surfaces for
life-sized subjects; but don't overlook the possibilities of the shop window
(See 59 C), chromium plate or any other highly polished surface.

A

B

A   SHIP-SHAPES
*The graceful lines of a yacht in
Cannes harbour prompted this picture
originally. A hazy day with disappointing
misty distances had us looking
round for something other than seascapes,
when the subject presented itself.*
TIP:
*there is no need to include the whole
of the reflected object. A small part
will prevent you from making just
a puzzle-picture.*

B   BOY REFLECTING
*These reflections are used as a
background for the real subject, the boy.
It was his curiously graceful attitude
that caught our attention. Hurrying before
he could fall from his precarious perch,
we took a few steps to one side to place
his dark hair neatly between the
reflected towers.*

C   ELEGANT VARIATION
*The late afternoon front lighting
in Central Park, with a gentle breeze
riffling the water, gave almost ideal
conditions for a reflection picture.
We chose this viewpoint to include
the two men in the foreground.*

A

B

A LOOKING GLASS
At first glance you might think that this had been printed upside down.
Very still water in this Bruges canal has produced an almost perfect reflection, although slight movement gives the game away round the edges of the buildings.

B TOPSYTURVY
The observant visitor to Amsterdam will constantly find himself compelled to stop and watch the ever-changing reflections in the many canals.
TIP:
note that the image reflected is always darker than the actual object. When taking the reflection only, this is a good reason for giving more exposure than when photographing the original scene.

136

C

C ABSTRACT
*Is this a red-hot toasting fork or some
top secret weapon cruising under water?
No, it is a reflection of some primer paint
on a bridge in Amersfoort. The rest of
the elements are vaguely recognisable,
but we prefer to think of the whole
as a kind of abstract.*

A GAUDY NIGHT

By day in Geneva you can occasionally
see a delicate rainbow on the
Jet d'Eau (See 33 C);
by night, thanks to the brash lighting
on the far side of Lac Leman,
you can be sure of seeing these giant
medal ribbons.

B ZIG-ZAG

A group of parked cars comes well down
our list of desirable camera subjects,
but we couldn't resist the odd effect
created by these particular ripples.
Compare with the still water in 136 A.

138

C DURHAM CATHEDRAL

The magnificent Norman cathedral is much photographed, and this view across the river is one of the most satisfying. The house, tiny in comparison, has great value in the composition by acting as a 'stop' at the point where the eye tends to leave the picture when following the converging lines to the left.

D UNDERNEATH THE ARCHES

The ancient Hospital of the Holy Ghost in Nuremberg was built over the city's main river, thus making it possible for the building's own 'ghost' to materialise in the blue Pegnitz.

TIP:

reflections apart, notice the small patches of daylight seen through the arches; where possible show this in bridges and similar subjects to prevent the openings looking like entrances to a sewer.

C

D

Isolate for Impact

See it simple – see it big

'Isolation' is much discussed in photographic circles,
both by professionals and serious amateurs. The real beginner
gives little thought to the matter, and is the loser for it.
Talking about pictures, isolation means freeing your main
subject from a distracting background, or from any surrounding
objects interfering with the central feature. Apart from
landscapes and similar scenes of broad general interest,
full of detail, most pictures will be improved and will gain
impact by the isolation of the main subject.
In our illustrations you will see that about half make use of
the sky for isolation; we have chosen these deliberately,
since it is one of the most convenient methods for you to learn.

A

B

A BEAUTY TREATMENT
We went by train from Copenhagen to Elsinore, to get pictures of the 'Hamlet' castle. We failed, because of the weather; but passing through the shipyards in our taxi we saw these two beauties. We cut out the surrounding clutter of cranes by moving in close, and concentrated attention on the side-by-side position and the strong colour masses.

B TRIUMPHAL ARCH
This is the other side of the Arc de Triomphe – not the one you see when you walk along the Avenue des Champs Elysées. Late afternoon sun spotlights the Arch while the stormy sky and strong foreground shadows heighten the dramatic effect.
TIP:
the Avenue des Champs Elysées runs roughly south-east to north-west; if you want to photograph the Arc de Triomphe from that side you should make it one of your first morning pictures for best light.

C SPACE TRAVEL
To the newcomer, cable-cars are one of the delights of winter sports; old hands at aerial travel board them like buses. Try to find a spot where one stands out against the sky, like this one at Seefeld, not too high for your camera, or out of touch with the evergreens.

C

A LONDON PRIDE

*It is only when the Englishman travels abroad
that he appreciates how the London Transport livery
brightens the metropolitan scene. You couldn't
see it much simpler – or much bigger – than this!*
TIP:
*you have endless choice and a perfect place to
stand, free from traffic menacing your unprotected
back, at Hyde Park Corner near
St George's Hospital.*

A

B WATER-TAXI

This picture was the result of a passing glance – and a second look that snapped us into action. We were just above the little pier, looking down from the Canzone del Mare in Capri; the impact comes from the colour and shape of the boat, the grouping of the people, and the low side lighting.

C VORTEX

This symbolic steel sculpture stands on its pedestal in Keukenhof Gardens. You are obliged to do a 'knees bend' to free it from background trees; don't overdo it, or you will distort the basic circular form to an ellipse.

D GOLDEN TOWER

This picture of the Grolier Building in New York has undeniable impact, but we only claim credit for keeping our eyes open. The evening sun happened to heighten and glamourise the normal golden colour of the tower; taking the picture from our viewpoint made a 'frame' of the foreground buildings. Noticing it was the main thing.

A FLAG DAY
The Norwegian flag flew in Paris to celebrate a royal visit. A low viewpoint at street level compelled us to isolate it against the blue sky; our contribution was to wait patiently until a lazy breeze found enough strength to lift the flag to a horizontal position.

B RED REAPER
Travellers ourselves, we know that many pictures are unplanned, and spring from the occasion. Driving to the Edinburgh Festival through Lincolnshire, we spotted this colourful corn-chopper from the road. Having watched its circuit, we chose a slope in Adam Duguid's field from where we could photograph the red reaper against the blue sky.
TIP:
try not to place a moving object dead centre in your viewfinder; leave room for it to 'move into'. The bus on the previous page is standing still, but even so would be happier with more space in front.

C PALAZZO PUBBLICO
This is the Italian equivalent of 'town hall', and the Torre del Mangia on the Palazzo Pubblico in Siena is 286 feet tall. It caresses the blue sky with its own slender grace; all the photographer has to do is select the right viewpoint and the right time of day, suggestions for both of which may be found in our picture.

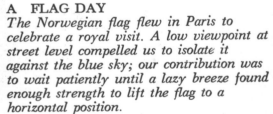

Strictly for Beginners
First steps to animation

We know that some of our readers, though veteran travellers,
may be camera novices. This section is included for their benefit.
We took for granted a certain degree of camera experience
in our section 'Markets' (pp. 20-25) and 'Candids' (pp. 44-49),
but beginners may find these beyond them. Although it is not
difficult to learn to work fast with a camera,
it will be best to practise on simpler subjects first.
Amongst the easy examples we show here, some have plenty of room
for the subject to move around, as in 'Pompeii' and
'Arrival Platform'; in others the movement is confined to a limited
area, as in 'Polar Bears' and 'Look – One Hand'. All the pictures
are better because they have animation in varying degrees.
A little practice along these lines, and you will no
longer point the wrong end of the camera at Elizabeth Taylor
if she unexpectedly walks past you in the Via Veneto.

A & B POMPEII
*Spend a moment comparing these two
pictures taken in the Forum at Pompeii.
The pensive young lady sitting alone is some
photographer's girl friend, wife or daughter.
We see this sort of picture taken year
after year – with the model posed like a
transfixed butterfly. In the other,
the young couple are strolling through
quietly enough, but they bring the picture
to life unmistakably. Any cine-enthusiast
would capture them without hesitation;
you can take them on an ordinary
35mm. camera with ease, and your result
will be a big improvement on the one with
the static figure.*
TIP:
*you will have converging verticals if you
take pictures like these from ground level;
to gain height we scrambled up on to
a piece of masonry like the one in
the foreground.*

A

B

C PARASOL PLAYERS
*Gillis Hag's trio plays in the open air
nearly every day of the summer
in Stockholm. We found them on
the esplanade of the City Hall. Look out
for an animated subject like this;
first adjust shutter speed and aperture,
then take your courage in
both hands and move in for a close shot.
(See also 29 D).*

A

A POLAR BEARS

This playful couple battling in their pool at London Zoo stir up a commotion which makes a perfect animation picture. This is easy to take because your subjects can't move out of range, and you are in command of the situation.

TIP:
this is a case where you don't want to see any blur; when your subjects are as active as this use a wide aperture and a fast shutter speed for safety.

B ALKMAAR

Members of the Cheese-Bearers' Guilds carry cheeses to the weigh-house. The colour of their glistening straw hats denotes the guild they belong to; and if you can get a man wearing a red hat with a blue-hatted partner carrying yellow cheeses on a green sledge you score a grand slam. We missed out on the colour of the rearguard's hat.

B

C

C PROCESSION

A walking subject is ideal for beginners' practice. In addition this picturesque group of the waif and her cow makes an interesting souvenir of Swiss local colour.

D ARRIVAL PLATFORM

Rapid action is not needed to bring a picture to life. In this quiet scene of the little fishing vessel making for port at Sorrento, the curving wake and the angle of approach clearly tell us that the boat is under way. Cover up the boat and see the difference.

D

A LOOK – ONE HAND!
*This is an easy subject for practice.
Let him go round a dozen times while
you get him in your sights, and then
take him when you're ready.
Don't take him broadside on; get him
just before, and you will have a margin
for error.*

B

C

B PERIOD PIECE
*Old Dobbin will never win the Derby
or the Preekness, but for our picture
in Disneyland he provides all the
animation we need.*
TIP:
*photographers in Disneyland will save
time and temper if they pick a spot
where the sun is right and let the vehicles
come to them, instead of chasing after
the vehicles.*

C COACH AND FOUR
*We found a place on the upper tier of the stand
at the Richmond Royal Horse Show so that we
could shoot over the heads of other spectators.
In front of them, against the railings,
we were much too close to the arena for comfort.
Our high viewpoint not only shows the coach and
team to advantage, but gives a good general
impression of the colourful throng of spectators.*

A

Bridges: Functional Beauty

'One more river to cross'

A country's art styles and social patterns are revealed as much by its bridges as by its churches and homes.
The little Dutch bridge (157 B) reminds us of Holland's struggle with the sea; in Venice (152 A) it is as much a part of the Renaissance as any church. Perhaps you have taken pictures of some bridges; you may have been disappointed in the results. It might be thought that the best place to take a bridge picture would be swimming in the middle of the river with a waterproofed camera, to see it broadside on; *aficionados* might even try this – but they will also be disappointed.
No, the best pictures will be taken from one side or the other at an angle carefully chosen to get the most telling perspective. We show you here some ways of doing this. Note the narrow angle used for the Aqueduct in Segovia, and compare this with the much flatter perspective used for Tower Bridge. Be advised by us – start with the smaller ones, and work your way up.

A VENICE
Visitors to Venice are sometimes disappointed by the Bridge of Sighs but never by the Rialto, for this world-famous bridge is more beautiful than any picture can show. Built in 1592, it must have been sketched, painted and photographed more times than any other bridge in existence.

B LONDON
Everybody has heard of Tower Bridge,
where the bascules are always raised when you want to drive over it, and never raised when you want to take a picture of it. Afternoon light is best for this view from the promenade, freely accessible to visitors, in front of the Tower of London.
TIP:
the bridge is opened for large ships which arrive or depart around high tide; if you want to show the bridge open, get to this spot about half an hour before (see daily press): you won't have to wait long.

B

A CHENONCEAUX

*This drawbridge over the château moat
could be raised to discourage the entrance
of the broker's man, but you can come in
at the main gate almost any time.
We scrambled down into the dried-up moat
to obtain a view of the solid foundations
of what is, after all, quite a small bridge
for pedestrians.*

B HEIDELBERG

*To capture the romance of Old Heidelberg
you will want to include the castle
standing on the hillside above the old town,
but you will find the castle in shadow
until late afternoon. Our sunset picture
perhaps overplays the romantic lighting
but shows the castle clearly.*

TIP:
*the Philosopher's Walk right above
where we were standing gives a
higher viewpoint from the same angle;
from there you will show a larger area of
the old town between bridge and castle.*

C SAN FRANCISCO

*Every visitor wants a picture of the
Golden Gate Bridge; few will get a good
one because it is so huge and because it is
almost always shrouded in mist.
Four mornings in a row we drove from the
Mark Hopkins without success; on the fifth
we got this at 10.00 a.m. from the roadside.
You may not park your car at
this standpoint; drop your photographer and
come back for him.*

D RIO DEI MENDICANTI

*There is no wheeled traffic in Venice,
all goods being transported by water;
those visitors who don't want to walk travel
the same way. This red brick and
white marble bridge near the famous
Colleoni equestrian statue is one of
the prettiest in Venice.*

E BADEN-BADEN

*A lively little stream called the Oos
runs through the heart of the town.
This is the prettiest of the bridges over it,
and people crossing often stop to look at
the golden carp in the stream. A short wait
and our picture was completed by these two
young ladies.*

C

D

E

A SEGOVIA

*Instead of crossing water, this bridge
carries it. You might not guess there is
a way through the Roman arches of the
aqueduct but for the little donkey
charging unflinchingly ahead. Because it is
so high and so long this is no easy bridge
to photograph; in this acute angle view
the perspective conveys an impression of
the length, and the tiny cart emphasises
the height. (See also 9 D)*

B EDAM

*'Lifting' bridges over the canals can be
seen in all parts of Holland; some are
simple structures like this one, while others
have a more ambitious layout.
All are well maintained as the bright
paintwork clearly shows, and we feel sure
you will want to have at least one in your
collection of Dutch exteriors.
(See also 199 C)*

TIP:

*with every lifting bridge you have the
choice of taking it closed, or open to
allow a boat to pass; here we preferred the
closed position showing the counter-
balanced arm isolated against the
blue sky.*

C DUBROVNIK

*Inside its walls it is a cosy little
place today, but 500 years ago this gateway
was a necessary protection against invaders.
The original drawbridge over the moat
has been replaced by this fine balustraded
stone affair, now that tourists have
become the only danger.*

B

C

When to Take it

A consideration of time and motion

You have to think about two aspects of the time element in deciding when to take your pictures. Our three illustrations of the Little Mermaid clearly show that the *time of day* can have a great influence on your result. Once you've learnt to notice the light changing during the day you cannot fail to take it into account.

The *other* time element is concerned with much shorter periods, ranging from minutes down to split seconds, in which you have to decide just when to press the button to get the best effect in pictures involving movement.

In two seconds the aircraft in the 'Munt Tower' would have flown right out of our viewfinder; in a longer period the tug in 'Day's Work Done' would have tied up at the dock.

In the first sense, the time of day, you are able to do some planning ahead; in the second, time of action, you have to think and shoot faster.

A

B

A MORNING
11.30 a.m. It has been said that the lighting is never ideal on the Little Mermaid at Copenhagen. Although it looks like a night shot, this one was taken in the morning. The result is mainly silhouette with the back lighting giving little more than splashes of highlight; the bronze figure looks almost black. A low angle enabled us to use the blue sky as a background.

B AFTERNOON
3.00 p.m. If your coach or guided tour brings you to the Little Mermaid after lunch, the lighting has changed. Then her back, legs and left arm are much more strongly lit, although the face is still in shadow; the bronze has now taken on a more natural tone. Photographed from a high angle, using the water of the harbour as the background.

C EVENING
5.30 p.m. The sun is already sinking fast, but this is the best frontal lighting of the day. The evening light has given us perhaps the most agreeable rendering of the bronze casting. Shadows are already creeping up the rock plinth, and there will soon be no more pictures. Taken at eye level, so that we see both sky and water in the background.
TIP:
if you can choose the time of your own visit to the Mermaid, go as late as you can; about half an hour before sunset is best.

C

A EAST IS WEST

*Tivoli's famous Chinese Theatre is normally
a hopeless subject for the visitor,
since the performances start after dark.
But this picture was taken at one of the
occasional afternoon shows during the summer,
which start at five. Enquire about them
when you get there.*

B DAY'S WORK DONE

*No single answer to the 'when' in this
picture will satisfy everyone. In our case,
we took three pictures of the little tug
coming home. In one it was further out,
and smaller; in another it was docking.
This is the one we like, with its feeling
of 'movement towards'.*

TIP:
*in Venice try to stay on the Riva
degli Schiavoni; this was taken from
our bedroom window – notice
San Giorgio Maggiore over the lagoon
in the background.*

C THE CANARY SHIRT
There may seem to be no timing involved in this view of the Santa Lucia port in Naples, but there was. We waited for the gentleman in yellow to make his third trip before we got him just where we wanted him.

C

D

D CABLE-CAR
Is it going or coming? It makes quite a lot of difference to the photographer. Just at this point, going up, it gathers speed – and may fool you. Coming down it slows, and you can place it nicely in your finder.

A

A MUNT TOWER
Aircraft arriving at Schipol airport near Amsterdam seem to home on this 17th century tower. Remembering that our own flight came in about 10.00 a.m. we stationed ourselves in a favourable position a little earlier to get this KLM plane and the tower together. You will have a wide choice from just before to just after ten.

B CARRIAGE DRIVE
There is so much coming and going at the Seville Fair that the photographer is in danger of using too much film because all the promenaders are so picturesque. In taking this long shot we found a vantage point on top of a fire engine. The problem was to choose the moment when groups of carriages moving in opposite directions made the street look busiest.

C PALAZZO INTO HOTEL
If a cat may look at a king, your authors may take a picture of the Royal Danieli. After choosing our viewpoint we waited for the gondola to move into our foreground. Pity it's empty.
TIP:
the façade of the palazzo, the stone bridge, the canal and the gondola make up a group which typifies Venice; keep an eye peeled for a concentration of features like this wherever you go.

B

A

A FIRST GLANCE

Tourists pass through the entrance to Hampton Court Palace, stop spellbound, and take this picture. The only one who gets any joy out of it is the cineman, who waits behind and takes all the other members of his party walking along the approach. The row of concrete posts doesn't make a very pretty picture, does it? And if you stand in the middle of the entrance you get two rows!

B SECOND LOOK

Nobody seems to stop halfway and take this shot. It still includes posts, a long foreground and uninteresting back views of other visitors, but the view of the Palace has improved. Things are looking up!

B

Where to Take it From

Above? Below? How far?
How near?

The last thing to do when taking
colour photographs is to press the
button; any thinking you do after that
is too late.
Some have no need to think; faced with
three different possibilities,
the extravagant man will shoot all three.
Some of us get more pleasure by
choosing in advance the one we think
to be right. Some of us never even see
the alternative.
One question you will have to consider
is how near or how far from the camera;
our three Hampton Court Palace pictures
will give you some food for thought.
A second question is whether the picture
can be improved by a camera position
above or below the subject.
There are far more occasions when
the high viewpoint will be an advantage;
consider 'Queen's Escort' and
'Slim Swim'.
Here's a practical suggestion.
The next time you are out with
the camera, take two pictures of the same
subject, trying out one of the points
we make here. You will learn far more
from your own demonstration pictures
than from any amount of reading.

C FINAL CHOICE
*The picture was taken with the same
lens as the first two. The great gateway
with its superb oriel window is obviously
a much more impressive picture than
either of the others. It is surprising
that few visitors stop for another shot
like this after taking the view from
the entrance. Always consider whether
there are other possibilities besides
the one you first thought of.*
TIP:
*many hostelries near famous tourist targets
are disappointing; the 'Mitre' at
Hampton Court is a notable exception.
Failing to have morning coffee,
lunch or tea at this historic inn
would be a blunder.*

C

A

A CITY LIGHTS
Our five days at the Mark Hopkins in San Francisco were memorable, but you need not actually stay there to get this picture or similar ones. The famous 'Top o' the Mark' cocktail room is available to all for the price of a drink; windows on all sides make it a photographer's paradise, with unforgettable views both day and night.

B STATE COACH
On a grey day in Munich we set off for the Schloss Nymphenburg, remembering to take a small flashgun and some blue bulbs, just in case. We decided to record the wedding-coach of Ludwig of Bavaria – but where to take it from? No room to get it all in, so we had to decide how much. In the end, to take a section which conveys the richness of the whole, we stood four feet away.

C QUEEN'S ESCORT
Her Majesty rides back to Buckingham Palace after the Trooping the Colour ceremony on Horse Guards Parade. Had this picture been taken from ground level it would be impossible to show the Guards in front and behind, with the crowds of spectators forming a frame for the Queen and her two escorts.
TIP:
because the Queen rides side-saddle she is naturally turned slightly away from our position on her right; you are more certain to be in a favourable position if you are standing on the side towards which she faces.

D & E GO UP - LOOK DOWN
Every city has a high point famous for its views, although many of them are disappointing for the photographer; some of the best views in Stockholm really are from the top of the Katarina 'Hisse', or lift. On a nice day, have coffee on the top terrace, or lunch in the smart Gondola Restaurant underneath it, identified by the yellow band in our picture. The traffic intersection known as the 'Slussen' is a good example of a subject photographed much more effectively from above. After our coffee on the top terrace, we managed to get five different forms of transport in our shot; boat, tram, bus, private car and lorry. We took a little trouble to get the Yellow Peril where he was most useful.

166

B

C

D

E

A OLD ATHENS
*For visitors to the Acropolis this is
the easiest imaginable shot to take;
but nine out of ten people who stand on
the edge looking over the 'Plaka',
where most of the amusing tavernas
are found, fail to raise their cameras.
Now let's see; landscape, seascape . . .
would this be a roofscape?*

A

TIP:
to the left and in front of the two
blue domes, do you see tables and chairs
on a flat-topped roof?
That is Vlacchos' well-known taverna;
dine there in the moonlight one evening
– and take it in colour from the
Acropolis the next day.

B SLIM SWIM
*From the terrace restaurant of the
Hotel Tritone, near Positano, you look down
on the bathing pool two floors below.
The angle of the sun had produced a
curious effect of spotlighting, which made
pool and parasols stand out from the dark
trees; probably we would not have noticed
this from the level of the pool below.*

B

More Candids

Further thoughts on shooting fast

You are walking down the Corso, Bond Street, Boul' Mich –
you see Mel Ferrer and Audrey Hepburn coming towards you,
thirty feet away. Your camera is in its case; they won't mind
if you take their picture. Will you get it?
Avoid being caught on the wrong foot; prepare for
any eventuality. Candids can be divided into two types;
those you are looking for, and those you come upon unexpectedly.
In the first case you are anticipating the event, in the
second you may be taken unawares.
Keep your camera ready for action. Focus on fifteen feet;
and on a sunny day, with film rated at 64 ASA, set your shutter
speed and aperture to 1/125sec. at f/11.
Everything in your picture will now be sharp between ten
and thirty-five feet from the camera.
When taken by surprise you may not need to make any
readjustment – and it might be the best shot of the day!

A

A YOUNGER GENERATION
When we ran across Kim Fich and
his pretty girl friend in Copenhagen
they were obviously having so much fun
that we asked if we might take
some pictures. 'Why not'? was the answer,
and they took no further notice of us.
Such a capacity for detachment is unusual,
and we like to think our
pictures are, also.

B TEENAGE PRIMA DONNA
Like all tourists we took the Circle Line boat trip round Manhattan Island; like many we found the weather not very good for ship-to-shore pictures. We made the best of a bad job by taking our fellow passengers, including this uninhibited coloratura entertaining her own friends.

B

C

C LITTERATEUSE
The newpaper-and-magazine kiosk is a fruitful corner in which to look for candids. Anxious business men, teenagers, stop-watch tourists, or, as in our pictures, an elegant young thing looking perhaps for Paris-Match; all make good candids.
TIP:
even a promising subject like this sophisticated lady will look better in action; wait for something like the hand raised to the magazine rack.

171

A QUANTO COSTA?
*Our svelte tourist bargaining unconcernedly
with the gondolier makes a custom-built
candid. Only by being inconspicuous can
the photographer hope to get in a number
of people without at least one of them
noticing him.*

B 'MIND YOUR BACKS'
*We took our photograph of the
United Nations Building (17 D)
from the Pepsi-Cola docks (by permission)
across the river. Leaving the plant,
we stopped to watch this fork-lift driver;
the bright orange runabout intrigued us,
and we waited for a moment when the
driver was turning to look behind him
before backing away.*
TIP:
*in such a scene it would a mistake
to shoot the machine when it was out in
the open yard, away from the surrounding
detail. The loading bay, the crates and the
lorry in the background all add interest.*

C SALT STACK
*On the beautiful drive from Athens
to Sounion you will see the salt flats
not long before you reach the Cape.
You might easily pass them without
noticing. If you go there, try to get a picture
of the men trundling their heavy sacks
along on the trolleys. The tiles protect
the great salt mounds from the rain.*

C

D 'HEARD THIS ONE?'
*An incident like this has the classic
ingredients for a candid. A small group,
an interesting setting, unawareness of
the camera and action visually clear
(the safety helmet is obviously telling
a new one about Pat and Mike).
Your problem will be to get near enough
to take your shot without attracting
attention and thus spoiling the
naturalness of the picture. We used
a medium long-focus lens.*

D

173

A THE WAITING GAME

*The Crillon, that high-class hostelry
for the high-class tourist, forms the background
for our Paris scene. Such a group caught
unawares offers a wealth of information.
The passengers don't stand in an orderly queue,
the long shadows suggest it is late afternoon,
the casual dress of the ladies indicates a spell
of fine weather, while the resigned attitudes
of the matelot and his girl friend show
that they expect a long wait for their bus.*

A

B

C

B IT WENT THATAWAY!
Our victims at the regatta were actually able to follow the progress of the race, although all we could do was admire the pretty boats and snatch surreptitious shots of the cognoscenti. We kept the horizon high in the picture space as we wanted to show the sea, not the sky.
TIP:
this picture gains in vitality because the three main characters all have their attention concentrated on one incident; learn to choose such moments for your candids.

C DOLCE VITA
Fugitives from the daily round make the most of the Mediterranean sunshine whenever they can; here they are doing it in Capri. The brown skins are always better targets for your camera than the newly arrived white ones; they will also be less camera shy.

They're Changing the Guard at Buckingham Palace

And you'll be there!

The world's most famous royal ceremonial, London's greatest free show, seven days a week, the year round. But will you get a good picture of it?
Probably not if you don't know:

When to go
Where to stand
What is going to happen

Let us help you. To be sure of a good view arrive half an hour before the advertised time of starting.* There will be plenty going on to keep you amused. Stand on the steps of the Victoria Memorial facing the Palace – and stay there! Don't be tempted to move by all the other things going on; you are in the best place for the climax, when the Old Guard complete with band marches through the great front gates. There are other ceremonial occasions in London; we show illustrations taken from the best vantage points – the Horse Guards Parade and the Mall.

* 11 a.m. weekdays; 10 a.m. Sundays

A MARCHING MUSIC
The drum and fife band of the St James's Palace contingent arriving at Buckingham Palace is one of the distractions which might tempt you to leave your position on the steps. Don't! If you want this picture, come again another day.

B GRAND FINALE
The Palace gates have been closed until this moment when the Old Guard, leaving the forecourt, turns to your left and marches off to Wellington Barracks. This is the Grand Finale which many visitors miss because they are not sure what is happening.

TIP:
wait for it; don't take the band just as it passes through the gate, but wait until it spreads out into a more impressive picture.

C EXEUNT OMNES
This is the last episode in the finale and if you missed the picture of the Old Guard marching away (B) you still have a chance to get this contingent.
It turns to your right and marches to St James's Palace to take up duties there.
In the foreground (left) the man's head has scarcely moved between the two exposures.

A IN THE MALL

The Royal Horse Guards (blue tunics, red plumes) and the Life Guards (red tunics, white plumes) do duty alternately at the Horse Guards in Whitehall. You can take them both on the same day if you stand half-way along the Mall at about 10.50 a.m.,* when the New Guard passes on its way to work. Forty minutes later the Old Guard passes in the other direction on the way to Wellington Barracks.
* 9.50 a.m. Sundays

B MOUNTED MUSIC

These two famous drum horses are the most valuable animals in the British Army. One belongs to the Life Guards and the other to the Royal Horse Guards; on rare occasions they are seen, as here, heading the combined bands of the Household Cavalry.

C

C SCOTS GUARDS

Swinging bravely along the Mall, these men
are identified by the thistles on their collars.
Although all the Guards wear bearskins, the visitor
can easily tell them apart by remembering the
thistle for Scots, shamrock for Irish, leek for Welsh,
star for Coldstream and grenade for Grenadiers.
TIP:
in any picture of marching soldiers, try to catch
the hands at the peak of the forward movement;
follow the rhythm for two or three paces
before shooting.

A MAJOR RODE AHEAD

This is a typical scene on many ceremonial occasions along the Mall. One minor difficulty is that the four Life Guards following the major all hold swords upright in their hands; taken at precisely the wrong moment all four faces could be obscured. The problem does not arise when they are returning in the opposite direction, as the faces are nearer to the camera than the swords.

B TROOPING THE COLOUR

The Queen's official birthday is celebrated on a Saturday in June by the splendid ceremonial occasion 'Trooping the Colour'. We hope you will be lucky enough to be there one day. In our picture the foremost rider is the Queen, inspecting troops during the ceremony. And don't ever say 'Trooping of the Colour' unless you want black looks.

C C.O.s
*Lieutenant-Colonels commanding the
Coldstream and Irish Guards riding along
the Mall. Apart from the badges on the
collars of their tunics, their regiments
can be identified by the colour of
the cockades in their bearskins.*
TIP:
*when taking any ceremonial pictures
in the Mall, always stand on the south side
with your back to the Park;
you'll have the sun where you want it.*

D HORSE GUARDS PARADE
*One of the special occasional treats
for visitors who watch the daily press
for such events. The Life Guards,
reminding us here of the Bengal Lancers,
are in manoeuvres on the occasion of the
presentation of new colours.*

Streets Broad and Narrow

Character study in highways and byways

A street is such a matter-of-fact, everyday affair . . . it starts at No. 1, and ends
where it finishes; we are so busy going from here to there we forget to look at it.
Your camera can give you a street from every town you visit, with its
character and local colour complete – from the Paris boulevard to the tiny
street in Dubrovnik, from Broadway to Pompeii, from Fifth Avenue
to the Grimsel Pass.
Our intimate street scene at the kiosk on the Champs Elysées (185 C) is a
cameo full of warmth and humanity; without exaggeration, you could take it
twenty times a day in Paris. It is a pity that most visitors will leave
without ever having photographed it at all!
Start now to collect a street, avenida, strasse, via, paseo or thoroughfare
from each town on your holiday journeys; you will be surprised
how quickly you learn to find the area where the concentrated flavour of
the town is to be found – in a street, broad or narrow.

A

B BROADWAY

In any one day, more taxis pass this spot in front of Gimbel's store than any other place in New York. They are garish and gaudy, and gave our camera hysteria as it tried to register improbable colours hitherto unknown.

TIP:
we found New York's big, bright taxis fascinating, but no more so than London's small, drab ones or Ischia's little three-wheelers. Why not start a collection of pictures of foreign taxis – one from each country you visit?

A AN DER HAUPTWACHE

The Zeil, in the centre, leads into the Hauptwache, the busiest traffic centre in Frankfurt. In London, watching traffic would seem to us a dotty diversion; but when we had coffee on the roof-top terrace in the middle of the Hauptwache we found the ever-changing scene engrossing.

C POWELL STREET

A visit to San Francisco without a ride on one of the famous cable cars is impermissible; the best is the Powell Street run, from Market Street below to Nob Hill above. Half-way up, pagoda-style towers on either side show that you are passing through one end of Chinatown.

B NARROW STREET
No cars spoil the peaceful atmosphere
inside Dubrovnik's walls, and you have
time to take your pictures without having
to jump for safety afterwards.
These 17th-century homes, with their
beautiful stone balconies, greet the
enterprising photographer who ventures off
the man streets – he may even find
a ready-made troupe of strolling players.

A CAPRI STREET
This winding lane leads into the Piazza,
just visible at the top. We chose for
our background the sun-faded red fronts and
the 'Tabacchi' sign, and stood with
the sun behind us in a spot where
visitors would pass in both directions.
All we wanted was a beauty queen or two
in bikinis, but they were in short
supply that day.

A

B

C CHAMPS ELYSEES

*This is the man our book is written for.
With camera slung on shoulder, wife and
child in tow, he is buying a paper from a
kiosk in the most famous street in Paris. In
the same street he could also buy a coffee
or a car, climb the Arc de Triomphe
or just sit and watch the world go by.*

TIP:

*don't be embarrassed about studying
the postcards on display at these kiosks –
we do it ourselves! You don't have to
copy them but they will certainly
suggest what to take and where to take
it from.*

A

A STREET OF ABUNDANCE
*This is surely the oldest of our streets,
just as the 'Strip' is the newest.
In Pompeii the Via dell'Abbondanza felt
the feet of passers-by two thousand
years ago – some time before we began to
worry about half-frame or coupled meters.
The ruins are full of camera subjects,
but we hope you will not forget to include
one of the little streets.*

B BLACK FOREST ROAD
*The road from Freiburg to
Donaueschingen, curving back upon itself
to follow hillside contours, is typical
of such Black Forest scenery.
From Baden-Baden southwards the forest
is most impressive, but far from easy
to photograph; you must look carefully for
a vantage point from which to take a bend
in the road, if possible.*

B

C

C THE 'STRIP'

It has nothing to do with a provocative night-club routine. It extends for four miles into the desert from downtown Las Vegas, with famous gambling resorts on either side. The 'Strip' is a challenge to the photographer. Where to take it from is only the first problem; 'when' is the second – we recommend that you do it at night. If you spend more time with your camera than you do at the tables you will thank us!

D GRIMSEL PASS

This is the only link between the lush Bernese Oberland and the comparatively sombre Valais. Newcomers are awed by it; old-timers take it in their stride. Don't leave your pictures until too late in the day or the western side of the gorge will be in shadow by four o'clock, even in summer.

TIP:
there are several places on this 7,000-ft climb where you can stop in safety to take pictures; ours was taken from the Spitallam Dam, high enough to give an impressive view along the valley.

D

OSEBERGSKIB

A

The Shape
of the Picture

Don't make them all horizontal

If it comes to that, don't make them all vertical either!
Because most 35 mm. cameras are more comfortable to
hold for horizontal pictures, there is a slight resistance
to turning them round for vertical shots. Users of the
growing number of half-frame cameras find the opposite –
the upright shape is easier to take.

Of course the deciding factor should be the subject
itself, not the comfort of the photographer. Look at our
picture of the Viking ship and ask yourself whether you
can visualise it as a horizontal; similarly, would you
expect to see our row of gables at Dinkelsbuhel as
a vertical? No, they just wouldn't work.

To users of both types the message is the same; make the
effort to use the camera in the position best suited to the
shape of the picture.

B

C

B SCENE STEALER
*Our natural gallantry seems to have deserted us;
we intended to take a picture of a pretty girl
with her pet, but wound up with a picture of the
pet and a pretty girl. We had never seen
a six-months-old fox cub before, and in the
excitement took our eye off the ball – and the fox
stole the picture. Even in the excitement
we didn't forget to turn the camera round
for a vertical.*

C FEATHERED FRIEND
*Obviously this could have been in our group of
close-up pictures, but it has greater value in
considering the shape of the picture. At the zoo,
as anywhere else, keep asking yourself, 'Is this
going to be a vertical or a horizontal?'
After a while you will find the camera positioned
correctly, almost of its own accord.*
TIP:
*separated from our subject by a wire fence,
we pressed our lens against one of the holes;
being certain that it was unobstructed by wire,
we didn't worry about netting being seen in
our viewfinder.*

A SHIPPING LINES
*Take it vertical – or leave it! Your shape is
not always dictated quite so forcibly, but if you
want to include the graceful curving prow of this
Viking ship in the museum in Oslo there is simply
no other way to do it. You still have to make use
of every inch of space available, and a very
junior Viking helps to give scale.*

A PARTHENONPAREIL
*Can you imagine millions of photographs
of one subject? You may be sure that literally
millions have been taken of the Parthenon
in Athens. The plateau slopes down from its
'good' side; going back for a full view you get
either converging verticals or a long
empty foreground. Our side view, fairly close,
is a useful compromise.*

TIP:
*from where we were standing the
widest wide-angle lens wouldn't get it all in;
don't worry about what is left out, but
concentrate on making the best picture
you can of what you see in the viewfinder.*

B VIEW WITH A ROOM
*In our section 'Planning Ahead'
we advised you to choose your hotel
room with an eye to pictures as well
as comfort. Taken from the same balcony
as illustration 132 D we show this one
just to drive the lesson home,
and to emphasise in addition that
skyscrapers are best taken in an
upright shape.*

A

B

C DINKELSBUHEL

We took this row of old houses in Dinkelsbuhel after we noticed that we could count twelve gables in line. The attractive crescent pattern comes from the slight staggering of each house along the street. Naturally, only a horizontal frame could be used for this.

C

A SAUNA SIGN

You have met a wood-carver from the Black Forest (118 B); here is a specimen of the carved signs to be found throughout the area. One of the lovely resort towns is Hinterzarten, where almost all the direction signs are lively little art works like this one. An obvious horizontal subject.

A

B

192

C SEAT OF GOVERNMENT
Certainly both 'shapes' are possible for your picture of the Capitol in Washington.
We decided to try for the whole frontage, but chose the wrong day; maintenance men were testing sprinklers hidden in the lawn where we were standing. Have you ever tried suing the U.S.A. for two pairs of slacks?

B EN MASSE
Bulb growers in Holland are only too pleased to let you photograph their blossoms, but don't like you to walk amongst them. Standing at one corner of a field as we were, a much stronger impression of its extent is given by taking a horizontal picture. The tulips running out of the edges on three sides leave something to the imagination; the field might be enormous.
TIP:
this is one of the few cases where we have used a very low viewpoint; the higher the camera, the more you can see the spaces between the rows of tulips, detracting from the effect of a solid carpet of flowers.

D NAPLES
We saw a chance to get this famous Naples 'galleria' in a picture with part of the San Carlo opera house, and stood on the fountain-base in the middle of the roundabout to take it. The sheet of water was used to fill in the sunless side of the frame, which clearly had to be vertical to suit these tall subjects.

Night and Day

Take a second look –
you may want another picture

Having booked a room for the night some tourists spend a pleasant evening sampling the food and wine of the country; others sample the night life, the theatre or the cinema.

Photographers could do worse than look again at some of the things they have taken during the day, and examine the possibilities for evening pictures of the same subjects.

You need not take them from exactly the same spot; sometimes the night view asks to be taken from another angle. Artificial light may reveal details hidden by shadow during the day; what was the central feature of the picture may become the accent after dark; identical twins may be indicated. Whatever choice you make the pictures will add variety to your slide show and give a well-rounded view of your visit.

A

194

A & B JOURNEY'S END

The clock on Shell-Mex House stands at eleven, indicating that this is a good time for daylight shots here. As in other Thames scenes, high tide gives a chance to get some river traffic in the foreground. The 'Discovery' is moored permanently in the heart of London as a reminder of Scott's epic Antarctic exploration, and is open to visitors.

In the night scene the clock shows ten minutes past ten. At this time of night it is remarkable to have so much daylight in the western sky, an indication that the picture was taken on a clear evening, very close to midsummer. A different viewpoint was used, giving greater prominence to the 'Discovery' as the treatment of the night shot is much broader, there being less detail to record.
The horizon was kept low in order to show the masts reaching up into the sky.

TIP:
with the comparatively long exposure needed at night there is a possibility of some movement showing in the masts of the ship as it sways on the moving water – beware of wind and passing craft.

B

C & D FORTRESS

The Alcazaba in Granada, one of the best remaining examples of Moorish fortification, stands magnificently squat, powerful and forbidding – an early 'deterrent' which must have warned off many an intending invader.

The size of the massive walls seemed self-evident, but we took care to include the tiny figure of the child playing in the centre, for scale.

The night shot was taken from exactly the same viewpoint (cf. leaves on tower, right) but included more foreground to reduce the area of blackness.

Note when in Moorish Spain: an Alcazaba is a fortress, an Alcazar a palace.

TIP:

the left end of this wall, just out of picture, ends uninterestingly with no tower. You can get it all in if you wish, but in such cases it is better to resist the temptation. By leaving our wall 'unfinished' we have allowed the reader to continue it in his mind's eye. You can often make your picture stronger by leaving something to the imagination.

A & B LION'S SHARE

The Maison du Roi in Brussels, taken across the Grand' Place, shows a long foreground mostly occupied by parked cars. To give some other interest more appropriate to the Gothic building, the silhouette of the lion was included. It is in shadow because it is sheltered from the sun by the Hôtel de Ville behind the camera.

At night the newel post is artificially lit and becomes much more a picture in its own right, with the buildings on the other side of the Place forming a background instead of being the main feature. The slight luminosity in the sky is not daylight, but the reflection of other city lights from a low bank of clouds. It was actually raining when this was taken, the camera being sheltered in a doorway; the wet streets reflect cars and lights, and avoid the monotony of empty blackness.
(See also 42 A)

B

D

198

A & B N.Y. PANORAMA

*Pictorially this view of New York,
from the RCA Observation Roof,
is more satisfying than any view from
the building the tourist will
probably visit first – the Empire State.
This picture includes the
Empire State itself, which cannot be done
if you are standing on it. Also you are
lower down by thirty floors and thus better
placed 'amongst' the skyscrapers,
although still not low enough as we say
elsewhere. (See 39 A).*

*Notice, in the night shot, that by
placing the Empire State higher in the
frame we have included more foreground.
This has allowed us to extend the
dramatic diagonal of Broadway to its
utmost – a feature which is quite missing
from the daylight version.*

TIP:
*if in spite of our warning you must try
for a daylight picture like ours, be there
before 10.00 a.m: the sun has left
the near side of the Empire State by then.
Phone the RCA Building about weather
conditions upstairs before leaving your
hotel; unless the condtions are given as
'excellent' don't go – anything less
is no good for pictures. Final warning:
we waited twelve days for ours.
Night shots, of course, are much easier.*

C

D

C & D BRIDGE ON THE AMSTEL

*The same subject but different viewpoints;
in fact the opposite sides of the
Meagre Bridge. Our daylight viewpoint
was selected to enable us to include
the moored boat as foreground interest and
to take advantage of the morning light.
By night the bridge looks the same
from both sides, but we chose the one
opposite the morning view so that we could
include the red of the Carré sign;
there was no similar colour note visible
from the other side. The sign helped
to relieve the dark night sky, and has its
own interesting reflection in the Amstel.*

199

Al Fresco

A glass of wine, a Baedeker and thou.....
ah, Blankenberghe were Paradise enow!

Two of the joys of travelling are the ease with which
the tourist acquires a thirst – and the widespread resources
for curing it.
On balance, especially in hot weather, towns are thirstier
places than the countryside. Fortunately the law of supply
and demand operates with its usual efficiency.
Provided the traveller has obeyed the injunction to take twice
as much money as he thinks he'll want, he needn't be dry
for long. This doesn't apply in Britain, with its own
special approach to the sinfulness of being thirsty outside
certain fixed hours.
Go ahead and enjoy your refreshment abroad, but don't
let your camera take a rest; it's always willing to work.

A

A   OSLO
The 'Pernille' is in the park beside the
National Theatre and is popular with
students from the University nearby. When
we saw Ulla Wolden and her friends having
tea, something told us our collection lacked
a picture of three pretty Norwegian girls.
We asked them to go on talking, and took it.
Ulla is the one in the middle.

C COPENHAGEN
*This café with its gay umbrellas in the
Town Hall Square has a long frontage where you
can see as well as be seen. If you get a table in
the sun you are likely to be the subject of a picture
taken by some photographer who has read
our sections 7 and 28.*
TIP:
*when photographing friends in an al fresco setting,
choose a café in the holiday mood; this one in
the Radhuspladsen has all the necessary elements:
impressive façade, gay sunshades, flowers
and colourful fixtures and fittings.*

C

B STOCKHOLM
*How many travellers, we wonder, bother to seek
out the cafés with special associations? Here,
for instance, at the top of the Kungsträdgården,
is the very special haunt of Stockholm's
bohemian youth; bare feet are de rigueur.
Fascinating to look in during the morning, and
again at teatime; you may discover that many faces
are the same – they've never left!*

B

201

A THE PIAZZA

*This might be any one of a thousand
holiday resorts in Italy. The sunshine,
the little shops, the newspaper kiosk,
the leisurely atmosphere, and above all
the terrace cafés – all, all familiar but
endearingly different to the visitor who
has discovered it for himself.*

TIP:

*this picture is worth studying for its
high viewpoint; taken from ground level
you would see the people at only the
first few tables. In such cases look
round for a balcony or stairway.*

B DISNEYLAND

*Let's face it – you won't get a cup of
tea at this fairground ride, but you can
get a good picture of the teacups from the
'Skyway' cable-cars passing above them.
Our publisher (to whom we raise our hats)
says we included it in this section only
because we like the picture.
Well . . . perhaps.*

C ZERMATT

*Before you can even think of ascending
the Matterhorn you have a long walk from
Zermatt to the aerial cableway.
This restaurant is happily situated as an
intermediate resting place, and while you
are drinking your coffee you can look at
the view and think about the strenuous
climbing ahead.*

D VENICE

Most of the people at these tables
couldn't care less if you told them the building
behind them was Sansovino's masterpiece.
After all, just sitting there with your 'caffè latte',
watching the strollers pass, looking across
the lagoon at San Giorgio Maggiore, and with
the Doge's Palace a stone's throw away
– isn't that enough without names and dates?

D

A COLOGNE
*Near any cathedral you will be able to
find a café where you can sit with some sort
of view of the building; only Cologne has
an open-air restaurant, large and well-
appointed, with room for several hundred to
admire the magnificent façade while
satisfying the inner man.*

C CAPRI
*There is a wonderful opportunity for the
thirsty photographer at the Canzone del Mare
– he can sip his drink and take pictures
of the swimmers disporting themselves in
the pool. We had other ideas and put both
bathers and drinkers in the self-same
photograph.*

B

C

B NEW YORK

It's hot there on a hot day, and the Rockefeller Plaza is as good a place as any for you to sit beneath a parasol, watch the flags flutter, meditate upon Omar Khayyám and take an occasional picture just to keep in practice.

TIP:
limp flags hanging indolently on their poles are no use to anyone; wait for a breeze to set them fluttering.

Your Background needs a Foreground

Don't let an expanse of water beat you

Throughout this book we repeatedly mention foreground interest when discussing our illustrations. We dealt with the principle at some length on page 68. We are not nagging; it is most important, and the novice who grasps its significance steps at once into the advanced class.

The problem is even more difficult when an expanse of water separates the subject from the camera. The empty foreground in 'The Lagoon' makes its own sad comment on its photographer's lack of perception.

The solution can be found in a variety of ways; in 'The Thames' the foreground interest is dominant, while in 'Trechtingshausen' it is most effective in spite of its smaller size.

Once you've learnt to look for it you won't find it difficult to bridge that gap, or fill that wide-open space, with something interesting in your foreground.

A THE RHINE – TRECHTINGSHAUSEN

We include this picture to show that sometimes a useful foreground interest may be two-legged; on such occasions a turn of speed could be useful, but nimble wits are better.
We had finished lunch, stepped down from the terrace, and saw the Vaterland nicely placed for our camera – but no foreground. A few quick steps brought our rival into the viewfinder; and we had the steamer, plus.

B & C THE LAGOON

Every visitor to Venice remembers San Giorgio Maggiore, spectacularly placed across the lagoon from the Doge's Palace. To be sure of identical Giorgios, we used a tripod for our twin studies; the first is plainly incomplete, while the second has been improved by the arrival of the gondola. You are better off than we were as you will not need a tripod. You are mobile, and can walk about to bring some desirable foreground-filler into the exact space where you need it most.
TIP:
there are few occasions when you will want your background in sharper focus than the foreground; normally you should focus on the nearest important object – in this case the gondola.

207

A

A MEDITERRANEAN
The name on the foreground interest clearly indicates where we took this. Looking across the arm of the sea to St Maxime, the 'Kyma', fitted out in period style, appears small and insignificant; but our red and blue boat and the 'Marilou' from Toulon form links in a chain leading the eye to it.

B THE THAMES
Taken from across the river, the Houses of Parliament inevitably have a wide stretch of water at the base of any picture. Some foreground interest is essential to give a sense of third dimension and to avoid the effect of a dull panorama. The observation platform on the South Bank has provided a strong note harmonising with the subtle tints of the distant buildings subdued by morning mists.
TIP:
pronounced straight lines near the edge of the picture should be treated with caution; frame your scene very carefully in the viewfinder to make sure that they are absolutely vertical.

C THE RHINE – ST GOAR

*The brilliance of the colours on the
far shore of the Rhine is often subdued
by atmospheric haze.
In just these circumstances we used the
bows of the 'Eider' with its cheerful flag
to add a touch of brightness to
an interesting landscape which lacked
enough sparkle for a colour picture.*

D STOCKHOLM HARBOUR

*Everybody goes to Riddarholmen to take
a picture across the harbour,
and the problem is the wide stretch of
water between you and the City Hall.
We found a position where the flowers,
the resting visitor and the berthed 'Diana'
with its bright flag blowing in just
the right direction, all provided
additional interest.*

A GRANADA

The Torre del Damas with its pool, in the gardens of the Partal, makes a natural subject for your camera. You will see most visitors taking it from the left of the lion, about half-way along the side. That way they get in all the loggia across the pool; but we prefer our angle view, which enables us to include the stone lion for – guess what?

A

B PLOCE BEACH
*You have already seen a very different view
of the old port in Dubrovnik (72 A);
we wanted this one especially to bring in
the 'Ploce' bathing beach. Taken from
the driveway leading into the Excelsior Hotel,
we searched for a standpoint which would fill in
the empty expanse of sea – and found this,
with the Agave cactus for good measure.
There's more than one picture in
any subject, indeed; can you find a different
one of the old port for yourself?*

C BAY OF NAPLES
*After ten days at Posillipo we despaired
of getting a picture of Vesuvius because of
constant haze. The attractive foreground provided
by these unselfconscious youngsters solved
the problem. The hazy view of Vesuvius becomes
acceptable when combined with the sharpness
of the bathers; in addition, the long gap between
the camera and subject has been bridged.*
TIP:
*you can drive on to the mole of the little
Sannazaro Harbour where we took our picture;
we chose a low viewpoint to foreshorten the
stretch of water between the bathers
and Mount Vesuvius.*

Buildings, like people, seem to want to be taken full-face, and often this
is not the best view or the one which most clearly reveals their true character.
This you will convey most effectively if you can find a viewpoint where your
photograph includes not only the front, but a side as well.
Buildings are gregarious and gather in clusters, taxing your ingenuity
to take good pictures of them. A high position, such as we found
for 'United Nations', will avoid the common defect – converging verticals caused
by tilting the camera. If you have to take your photograph from a very acute
angle because the view of the façade is restricted, as in 'Alms-Houses',
try to include a balancing feature on the other side of your picture.
All our illustrations emphasise the need to avoid the full-face portrait
if you are trying to make a character study.

Buildings
not Frontages

Give them a third dimension

A

A CHAPEL
*When you are in Mykonos your pictures must include one of the chapels and one of the windmills. You will have to search for your windmill (p. 133),
but the chapels are everywhere. Most of them are commemorative, belonging to single families who have lost sons, fathers or brothers at sea.*

B OLD THEATRE
Epidaurus is the most famous and well-preserved of all the Greek theatres. In the summer, audiences of 14,000 from all over the country attend performances, as they did twenty-five centuries ago. Our view from the 'gods' shows the theatre in the round, with the original circular acting area. It cannot convey any idea of

C TOWN HALL
Adapted to later needs by combining three Renaissance patrician houses, the Town Hall at Freiburg-im-Breisgau presents a special photographic problem. The narrow street on the left leaves no room to manoeuvre, but we made the best use of space for a corner shot which would show off the handsome oriel window.

the phenomenal acoustic properties; from the top row you can hear a coin dropped on stage – we tried it.
TIP:
we are sorry, but if you want to show the full extent of the bowl you must climb up to the back row; the lazy man's view from stage level will only show about one-seventh of the circumference.

C

A

B

C

A COTTAGES
Believe it or not, this little group of houses in Penshurst, Kent, is known as Leicester Square – a very different setting from the other one. By taking a slight angle view we have hidden the shady side of the courtyard and emphasised the half-timbered fronts on the other. The red-tiled roofs and the blue sky needed no help from us.

B CHALET
This colourful flower-decked hotel is typical of the buildings seen in the Bernese Oberland, just as the people equipped for climbing are typical of the area in summer; in winter they would have skis. The name Fiescherblick refers to a view of the well-known peak, the Fiescherhörner.
TIP:
a 'perspective' view of a frontage like this usually leaves an unsatisfactory empty space on the opposite side of the picture; try to fill this space with a group like our climbers.

C NEW THEATRE
This oblique view shows the full beauty of the curved façade of the Stadt-Theater in Mainz, an effect which is lost when seen from the full-face position. Flowers and shrubs in large pots helped to fill a foreground which would have been stark without them.

D

E

D ALMS-HOUSES
In southern Germany, let nothing keep you from visiting the 'Romantische Strasse', which includes Augsburg. One of the city's proudest possessions is Europe's oldest group of alms-houses, the 'Fuggerei'. Your best light is about mid-day; try to include a little of the buildings on the left to add depth to your picture.

E LINCOLN MEMORIAL
A classic corner view of this classic style edifice in Washington. You might say to yourself, on looking at this: 'That's not so clever how else could you take it?' The truth would surprise you; we see photographers taking direct frontal shots of such buildings all the time!

A & B UNITED NATIONS
*In many pages we could not have told
the 'frontage' story as clearly as in this
pair of pictures. The tall Secretariat
Building is seen directly from the front;
striking, perhaps, but with no indication of
its depth – is it ten yards from back*

A

to front, or a hundred? In the other picture we see its true size and shape, and also its dramatic relationship to the General Assembly Hall in the foreground. If you want to see how these two shots come out in your camera, the full-face was taken from the 42nd Street fly-over between First and Second Avenues; the other from the IBM Building across the way. *Different and better standpoints you may find; we can assure you that you won't find them at street level.*

TIP:
if you are a bona fide amateur you may ask to go out on to the terrace of the Chase Manhattan Bank diagonally opposite. *We made the mistake of saying we wanted the picture for a book. Who said honesty is the best policy?*

Evening Light

The hour before sunset
for a romantic touch

Towards evening, sunlight becomes a warm golden hue which colour film notices instantly, although we ourselves may overlook its first traces.
At this time shadows lengthen as the sun sinks to the horizon;
the lighting is softer and pleasanter than at high noon but the larger shadow areas may be troublesome. In some pictures, notably portraits, you may find that the colours are too rich for your palate, so don't expect every exposure to be a winner. Keep your camera at the ready, however, as you may find some incident like our 'Lone Sculler' worth recording, or a sunset that takes your breath away.
When light is fading fast watch exposure details carefully,
and if shutter speeds fall below 1/125sec. take precautions to avoid camera shake.
You don't have to pay overtime rates to your camera – keep it working until it is time for it to sign on for the night shift.

A LONE SCULLER
Photography had finished for the day when we saw this lone sculler on the Keizersgracht in Amsterdam; we waited until she reached a pool of sunlight for our picture.
A wild guess at exposure
and a shutter speed we thought too slow for the subject surprised us by giving an acceptable result. After that we put the camera away.

B BRUGES BACKWATER
The first impression of visitors who see buildings growing straight out of the canal is that they must be damp places to live in. When they have recovered from this jolt, they begin to look for the most attractive 'canalscape' – a difficult choice where so much is picturesque.

C SUNSET SILHOUETTE
Sunsets are irresistible, and you will certainly try one sooner or later. We found ours in St Tropez, looking across the port to the Môle du Portalet, and waited until the sun was just sinking behind the distant mountains. The foreground silhouettes are typical of colour shots taken directly into the sun.
TIP:
when taking sunsets try to judge the time when the sky colours are at their maximum intensity; be careful – the duration is much shorter than you think!

A

B

B GLASS AND STONE
The modern skyscraper architecture of the building known as No. 2 Broadway is contrasted with the ornate, squat traditional of the New York Custom House. The four statuary groups in front receive sunlight only late in the day, which compels you to use evening light for this shot.

A GRANDEUR THAT WAS ROME
*Your local camera club will expel you
for taking the Colosseum from street level –
and you'll get a poor picture anyway.
Try the splendid raised terrace, a hundred
yards long, across the street. There you can
find a wide choice of camera positions,
but will still need the late afternoon sun
to cover the unbroken side.*

C SKYSCAPE
*Coming from Dinkelsbuhel on the
'Romantische Strasse', you see this view
of Rothenburg before reaching it.
We stopped by the roadside to take this
at about teatime; a horizontal picture
showing more of the town was tempting,
but we made this vertical to include
the lovely sky and clouds.*

C

D DISCUSSION GROUP
*Painting, politics, love and literature
seem to be the staples of the floating debate
in Washington Square on Sunday evenings.
The Greenwich Village intelligentsia form
into groups, dissolve into fierce tête-à-têtes,
or in threesomes examine – will you
believe it? – Douglas's Social Credit.*
TIP:
*even in a 'grab shot' you must try
to think of the background; we centred
the girl in the arch, knowing that her two
listeners would relieve a placing
otherwise formal.*

D

221

B

B HAT TRICK
In the town of Rhodes, all visitors wander down to the Mandraki Port for an aperitif before their evening meal. Seen from one of the many quay-side cafés, these three mills on the ancient mole are a conspicuous landmark. Side lighting accentuates the roundness of the stumpy structures.

A CARAVEL
We were told that this yacht is built on the style of the vessels which took warriors to the Crusades. We have our doubts, so have called it 'Caravel', a romantic if equally unauthentic description. But we like to think of the sunlight gilding its sails again.

C LAKE GENEVA
Sightseeing boats on the lake make numerous calls at picturesque piers like the one at Pully. With a car, you can take a picture at one pier, drive along the shore, and photograph the same steamer at its next stop.
TIP:
this pastime must take place on the north shore of the lake and you will therefore be looking into the sun most of the day; your best pictures will be taken in the afternoon.

C

223

People in Pairs

More trouble—but more amusing

Man is a gregarious animal and when you are out hunting him with camera he is most likely to be found in small groups consisting frequently of one male and one female. Your quarry can be stalked and caught unawares or can be warned before shooting. We show examples of both methods, each time trying to get away from the both-on-the-same-level appearance, but making sure that neither person steals the picture from the other.

If one is taller ('Montana Maid'), or is placed higher than the other ('Royal Guard'), it is easy to avoid a monotonous side-by-side effect. Another way of handling two specimens is to have one more full-face than the other.

A picture of two isn't *automatically* twice as good as a picture of one. You need to take extra care when shooting people in pairs.

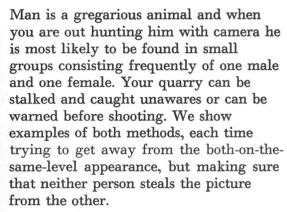

A   BRIEF ENCOUNTER
This promenade near Notre Dame is a favourite place for office workers to eat a sandwich lunch, for tourists to relax, or for layabouts to lay about. Our pair might be making a date, just gossiping, or doing a slow fox trot; their near neighbour couldn't care less – he's contemplating a crossword clue in Le Matin.
TIP:
a little cameo like this is as much a part of your Paris collection as Notre Dame or the Arc de Triomphe; try to record the living present as well as the historic past.

B   MORNING BATH
English students camping out in the foothills of the Matterhorn freshen up at this log, hollowed out for a drinking trough. Constant cold water adds to the amenities, although it is sometimes necessary to step out of the bathroom to make way for a thirsty cow.

A

A 'WHY SPANISH?'
*For some time we watched this couple
at the foot of the Spanish Steps. From the
amount he read to her they must know a
lot about Keats' House, the church of
Trinità dei Monti and the 137 steps
themselves. People in amusing and human
poses like this will add greatly to the
interest of your pictures.*
TIP:
*the artist painting the Spanish Steps
can leave out all the overhead wires;
the photographer, alas, is stuck with them.
We avoided all but one by settling for
half the width of the steps, and moving
in close.*

B TWO ON THE TARMAC
*We would rather miss a plane than
a picture. We dropped everything except
the camera when we saw this picturesque pair
walking towards our aircraft ahead of us
– and caught them unsuspecting in this
space-age setting of Phoenix Airport.*

C CARDBOARD CAVALIERS
For the 'Weinfest' in Braubach-am-Rhein local worthies dress up in 1815 uniforms to take part in the goings on. It's a thirsty business, and we found this colourful couple restoring their energies after the parade. We can vouch for the restorative properties of the local wine.

C

D

D MONTANA MAID
With the Capitol dome in the background, these steps have been the setting for more pictures than you could bear to look at. Congressman Battin of Montana poses here with a constituent, Williamette Youpee, the tenth Miss Indian America. Almost any summer morning you will get a Congressman in your sights on this spot; he will be eager to succumb to your blandishments.

E STANDING ROOM FREE
Sunday afternoon is the time for parades along Fifth Avenue, just the part of the day for sunlight to shine on the backs of the marchers – and leave their faces in shadow. Frustrated in photographing the procession, we turned our attention to the spectators – and found them every bit as interesting as the passing show.

E

A CAMERA CONSCIOUS

On our last visit to Venice a costume epic
was being filmed in the Piazzetta. We
spotted a path taken in twos and threes by
artists going to be made up, chose these two,
and called out as they passed. The result is
a happy compromise between a posed picture
and a candid – and successfully shows off wigs,
beards and rich costumes.

B ROYAL GUARDS

You will find it difficult to take a
'candid' of guards on duty before a palace.
If they're on duty, they're awake and
making sure that what you point at them
is only a camera. We asked politely
if we might take this shot of the Evzones
at the Royal Palace in Athens,
and permission was smilingly given.

A

B

228

TIP:
where there are military or police guards, it is wise to make sure that photography is allowed; if your film is confiscated you will lose not only the picture you shouldn't have taken, but all the others as well.

C CILIPI MEN
Unlike the Sunday-go-to-meeting dresses of the Cilipi ladies (49 B) these trousers are for everyday wear. We found this view enchanting; unaffected by Admass civilisation, their clothing seems to convey the local spirit of rugged independence. And as for 'pairs', isn't this more amusing than it would have been with one man?

C

Cathedrals and Churches

Easy to look at – hard to take

Cathedrals are amongst the foremost tourist attractions, and not without reason. Some are historic, some are architectural gems, some are monuments to the vision of one man, all represent the spiritual aspirations of mankind.

They are not among the easiest subjects for you to take, mainly because of their great size. Often there isn't enough space round them for pictures, and you have to be satisfied with a part as at Seville; others, like Sacré Coeur and the temple at Sounion, stand on high ground which makes a looking-up view unavoidable; most have the main entrance and west front, traditonally the architectural showpiece, in a position where they are best seen by late afternoon light.

We have shown some of the solutions, but each one is a separate challenge and you will have to use your own ingenuity to overcome the problems you encounter.

A

A ST PETER'S
*Pilgrims and tourists visit Rome in
thousands and all of them go
to St Peter's. With two fountains
and an obelisk in the great Piazza,
the pictorial permutations are endless.
We chose a position including one fountain,
one of the Bernini colonnades, the dome
and part of the Vatican, as a change from
the more conventional view 'straight
down the middle'.*

TIP:
*here are two tips for the price of one;
(a) this is a morning shot – the great
façade is in shadow by lunchtime; (b) if
you can be there by 9.30 a.m. you will
have half an hour of comparative comfort
before the coach-loads descend upon you.*

B SEVILLE
*The second largest church in Christendom
has no standard frontal camera position;
the buildings on all sides are too close to
permit a good general view. The most
rewarding outside detail is the flamboyant
Gothic south porch. Taken during
the Spring Fair, our picture shows one
of the many horseback couples to be seen
riding round the city all day long.*

B

231

A

B

232

A SEGOVIA

Circumstances forced us to take our pictures of this magnificent cathedral in the morning, when we tried to make the most of the light from the south. This view, different from the more usual aspect from the opposite side, was taken from the town square, where the bandstand steps provided a useful platform to raise us up a little.

TIP:
don't underestimate this fascinating town; it has one of the finest cathedrals in Spain, one of the best Roman Aqueducts still standing, one of the most famous castles in the world – and a dozen Romanesque churches as well! It's an amazing place.

B NOTRE DAME

Any day in the Place du Parvis Notre Dame you can see a demonstration of the difficulties of photographing this great cathedral. Tourists go further and further back until the cars parked round the square cut off their retreat. By this time they have a long foreground with the building in the top half of the picture. We solved the problem for ourselves by putting two friends near the lamp-post and waiting for some more visitors to walk through the middle distance.

C LINCOLN

Photographers, especially amateurs, tend to take the standard frontal view of cathedrals where possible; this familiar presentation has its value – we show some examples ourselves – but yours can be different if you wish. Here is a little-known view of Lincoln, taken from the Vicars' Court. No single shot can convey the personality of a great cathedral; extra vistas like this help to tell the story.

C

233

A GRINDELWALD

Our hotel on the right overlooked this local church, nestling between mountains at the end of the road. In the morning we waited for the sun to rise just high enough to spill over on to our side of the mountain and found another visitor with the same idea as ourselves taking a similar picture.

B PHILERIMOS

You have already seen one picture taken in this pretty spot in Rhodes (p. 127). This is another of the ancient monastery buildings, somewhat restored after the war. Getting three staircases in one picture would have been worthwhile, even with a less charming subject.

C SACRÉ CŒUR

This is another of the not-very-easy-to-take cathedrals. It stands high on the hill of Montmartre and the most impressive approach is up this stairway, although those who feel the burden of their cameras can go up in a funicular at the side. We have given some interest to the foreground by including several other visitors.

TIP:

rare amongst cathedrals, the main entrance faces not west, but south; try to make your visit to Sacré Cœur in the morning, before the sun leaves this face in shadow.

D

E

D FREIBURG-IM-BREISGAU
*Freiburg's famous pinnacled tower
was encased in splints, so we contented
ourselves with this composition based upon
the east end. A high viewpoint was
needed, and the genial proprietor of the
'Goldner Engel' opposite gave us access
to a front window on the top floor above
his restaurant.*

E ST ANTON
*Countless thousands of visitors to the
famous winter resort know this little church
on the outskirts. Being basically a
white subject, it is not an obvious choice
for a colour picture; but we liked the
strong diagonal of the mountain behind,
and the dark onion-shaped dome standing
out against the sky.*

235

Identification Built In

Give some of your slides an extra use

If you really wanted to, you could buy title slides to precede your selections of the foreign countries you visit. More creative and more individual is to collect your own on the way, especially if they are not completely straightforward and obvious.

We show both kinds; 'Vertical Take-off' couldn't refer to any country but Switzerland, and 'Pointed Reminders' clearly introduces Belgium. On the other hand, a picture which carries somewhere the words 'Seefeld' or 'Musée Fragonard', for instance, is likely to mean more to you in the years to come than many others in your collection.

You won't forget to take a picture of St Peter's unless you're terribly absent-minded, but if you don't keep an eye open for them as you go along you may easily overlook your built-in identifications.

A TIME OUT
Perhaps not to everyone's taste is a picture of a ski-park. What impelled us to take this one was the small 'Seefeld' sign, which alters the character of the shot. If the viewer knows Seefeld he will identify himself with the picture. Even if he doesn't, he will know the scene was taken in the Tyrol and not the Trossachs.

236

B

C

B NEXT STOP NAPLES
*The national flag, the ship's name,
the port of registration – Napoli,
and other signs all add up to the
Italian flavour of this scene of passengers
disembarking at the quay in Ischia.
If you are interested you can also deduce
that it was taken in mid-morning, as the
time of return is 11.10.*
TIP:
*try to take people leaving the boat
rather than embarking. They tend to go
aboard in ones and twos; disembarking
they are grouped more compactly and
make a better action picture.*

C SIGN OF THE TIMES
*We took this picture in Washington
during the summer of 1964 because we admired
the spirit of the round-the-clock crusaders.
Subsequently we realised that its
built-in message made it a perfect
illustration for this section in our book.*

A VERTICAL TAKE-OFF
*A sign of this type is an obvious subject
for a title slide; everybody seeing it
would know at once that the theme
is Switzerland. Although we found this
full sized identification in Lausanne, you can
make you own selection; park well
away from dangerous road junctions.*

B PAINTING NOT PERFUMERY
*Besides being the famous centre for
perfumery in France, Grasse houses in
its museum a collection of the works of Fragonard
and other Provençal artists.*

TIP:
*your friends might think that such
touches of local colour add
interest to your slides; the picture
becomes more than just another
street scene.*

C

D

C OLDE WORLDE
Just in case it might be thought that this is the junk pile in some forgotten corner of a farmyard, the yellow sign informs us that it is an open-air antique shop, which prompts a second look. Then it is noticed that the farm vehicles are well-preserved collectors' pieces. They can be seen a few miles from Concord on the road to Boston, Mass.

D SERVICE RAPIDE
If you ever drive along the South Coast from Marseilles to Nice, try to spend a day on the Ile de Porquerolles, that idyllic spot of beauty and tranquillity. Instead of the beach scene you might expect to see, we show you here the little pier with its built-in identification. We forgot to ask what the 'B' stands for!

A

B

A DANISH PASTRY
Dare we include a picture just because it brings back happy memories of Copenhagen? We dare, and perhaps you too will go for your morning coffee at the Café a' Porta in the Kongens Nytorv. Then you will see why we wanted this souvenir.

B POINTED REMINDERS
On the outskirts of Bruges the evening sun spotlights nine direction signs which remind us that the Belgians still persist in using their very own spellings of place names which seem odd to the visitor. Not to worry – they still refer to Londres!

C NEAT BUT NOT GAUDY
One of the most celebrated hotels in the world, the Waldorf-Astoria gives us a taste of its quality in the Park Avenue entrance. This is a double-identity case; first, the carved and gilded inscription over the doorway, and second, the flag of Saudi Arabia indicating that King Faisal was staying in the hotel at the time.
TIP:
the blending of the taxi paint job with the green and gold of our main subject is no accident; we waited – not long – for the right one to stop at the cab rank.

c

Extending the Season

Stretch it at both ends

Colour photography is a game you can play all the year round. Don't put your camera away in a cupboard somewhere and forget all about it until you are off on your next holiday. If you do, the half-used film you left in it may be out of date. At least finish it up first, and discover that some autumn pictures may be the start of a new pleasure which can continue throughout the winter. Of course the winter holiday-maker has unrivalled opportunities on the ski-slopes – and après-ski! He will almost certainly have good light as well. But stay-at-homes can find endless subjects in museums, like our 'Sleigh Belle' or 'Pas Seul'.
There's no closed season at all, and your Christmas pictures will be better if you've kept your eye in.
Once you've extended the season by continuing into the autumn and starting early in the spring, you will soon learn to make both ends meet.
Don't let your camera hibernate!

B EXTERIOR DECORATOR
Travel is reputed to broaden the mind, and one discovery we made was that Delft pottery is only blue after it has been fired. To prove this we took a flashlight picture of an artist painting a design on a large vase, copying the detail from a finished article. Subjects like this are waiting for you, in any city, all the year round.

A CROCUS CARPET
Londoners look for brighter days ahead when they see the first crocuses in Kensington Gardens from the top a No. 9 bus. The pallid sky and the long shadows are typical of early spring in London. Any Cockney could tell you that this was taken in April.
TIP:
misty atmosphere always subdues colours in the distance; in such conditions try to get a bright note in the foreground where it will not be affected by haze.

C

C FIND THE LADY
And you might have trouble without help,
for even the 'Queen Elizabeth' looks small,
seen from New Jersey across the Hudson.
Taken from the home of our Weehawken friends
the Ellenbogens, the picture shows
the veiling effect of autumn mists;
colours subdued, contrast softened
– and an attractive unsubstantial quality
differing from the harsh reality
of summer sun.

A

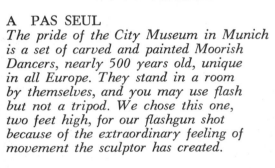

A PAS SEUL
The pride of the City Museum in Munich is a set of carved and painted Moorish Dancers, nearly 500 years old, unique in all Europe. They stand in a room by themselves, and you may use flash but not a tripod. We chose this one, two feet high, for our flashgun shot because of the extraordinary feeling of movement the sculptor has created.

B

B SUMMER IN NEW YORK
We were startled to find that the ubiquitous hole-in-the-road appears even on Fifth Avenue. Standing by St Patrick's Cathedral, we lost no time in getting the evidence on film, taking care to include the 'caution' sign, some workmen, traffic dislocation – and the hole!

C WINTER IN THE TYROL

*Some have winter thrust upon them;
others spend time and money to reach it.
The photographer born in Seefeld takes
pictures in Capri or Majorca; we couldn't
wait to get this shot of the Ross-Hütte
above Seefeld with the peaks of the Tyrol
rising behind. A spot of red always helps
a little, as you see.*

TIP:

*sunshine with snow may be common in
Austria, but in Britain it is rare; wherever
you are, always take advantage of this
combination to get some winter pictures
with summer sparkle.*

D SLEIGH BELLE

*After taking Ludwig of Bavaria's
bridal-coach (166 B), we turned to the
golden winter sledge made at the same
time. It was raining outside, so we had
plenty of time to chose the detail we
wanted – this charming gilded mermaid
lighting the sledge's way through the snow.*

C

D

A CHRISTMAS CARD
*Winter sunshine and snow in Latimer,
Bucks; the seasonable feeling is completed
by the bare branches. There are no people
about; only the photographers hadn't enough
sense to go in out of the cold, because they
couldn't resist the sight of a blue sky
and sunshine in an English winter.*

B OLD GOLD
*With winter frosts before us, we look
nostalgically at these glowing reminders of
summer just past, and make trite remarks
about the days drawing in. These
particularly fine autumn leaves were found
at Freudenstadt in the Black Forest. Sunlit,
and backed by a blue sky, they make a
romantic picture of autumn.*

C HAIL AND FAREWELL
*In choosing the four-hundredth and
final illustration for our book we decided,
like old-time magicians, to go out in a flash
of flame. These particular flashes of flame
go on from early spring to late
autumn in Copenhagen's Tivoli Gardens. We
took our pictures in comfort from the open
terrace bar on the twentieth floor of the
Royal Hotel just across from the Gardens.*
TIP:
*you will need a tripod for successful
pictures of fireworks. Use the viewfinder
to select a likely area for effective bursts;
then open the shutter, at the 'B' setting,
with a cable release. You don't have to
close it after the first display – our picture
is made up of two separate bursts.*

A

B

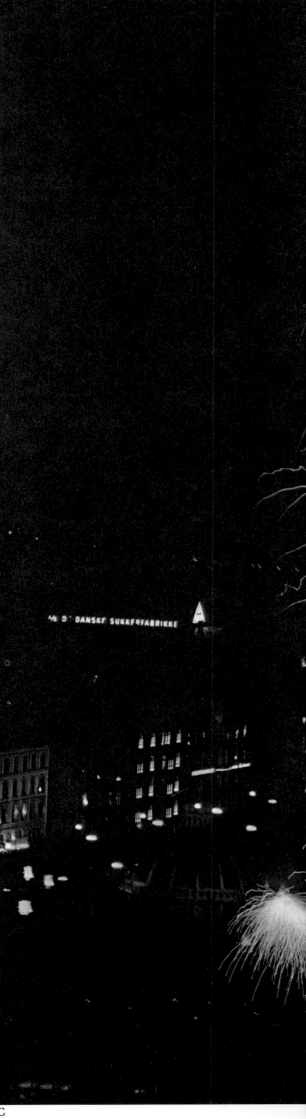

C

Places Index

251

Subject Index